IBM 14940

DATE DUE

THE SPORTS OF OUR PRESIDENTS

THE SPORTS
OF OUR
PRESIDENTS

by John Durant

HASTINGS HOUSE PUBLISHERS

NEW YORK

*This book is written for the young in heart —
and such a one is Alice Kobbé Rand,
to whom it is dedicated.*

Published simultaneously in Canada
by S. J. Reginald Saunders, Publishers, Toronto 23.

Library of Congress Catalog Card Number: 64-13482
Printed in the United States of America

* This book follows the *Encyclopaedia Britannica* and the *Chicago University Manual of Style* in the use of the capital P when referring to the President of the United States.

Contents

THE SPORTS OF OUR PRESIDENTS

WASHINGTON AT THE AGE OF TWENTY-FIVE.

From a miniature on ivory presented by Washington to his wife Martha and now belonging to her daughter's family

I am Sir Yr Most Obed.t H.ble Serv.t

Fort Loudoun
10.th Sept.r 1757

G: Washington

Washington at the age of twenty-five.

CHAPTER 1

The First Sportsman of Virginia

GEORGE WASHINGTON was first in about everything he did. As a boy he was first across the finish line in foot races with his playmates, and hardly anyone could beat him at tossing heavy weights for distance or at jumping with the long pole.*

All his life he was among the first — a leader and a trail blazer. He was only sixteen when he rode off across the Blue Ridge Mountains of Virginia on the first surveying expedition ever made into that wild country.

He spent three years on the frontier among the Indians, until surveying became too tame for him and he decided upon a military career.

His rise was rapid in the Virginia militia. At the age of twenty-two he was a full lieutenant colonel and was the first to lead Virginia troops in battle against the French and Indians.

Later, in our struggle with the British for independence, Washington became the first commander-in-chief of the American armies. Still later, in 1789, he took the oath of office as the first president of the United States.

Light-Horse Harry Lee, a brilliant cavalry commander during the Revolution, was a congressman in 1799 when the news of Washington's death saddened the country. The old cavalryman rose

---

* A broad jump with the use of a pole to give greater distance on the ground, rather than a pole vault aiming for height.

to his feet in the halls of Congress to pay tribute to the Father of his Country.

"First in war, first in peace and first in the hearts of his countrymen," said Light-Horse Harry Lee of his beloved leader. The words still ring clear through the corridors of history. However, they do not include another field in which the great man was supreme, nor do most history books mention what this was.

It was sports and out-of-doors activities. He was foremost in this field, the first of several sports-loving presidents who followed him. No president, though, was more of a sportsman than our first one. Only one or two could come close to being his equal.

A born athlete, he was strong and muscular all his life. Even in his boyhood he had enough power in his arms and shoulders to handle the most unruly horse with ease.

A well-known story told about him by many historians shows how strong and daring he was in his early years. Young George, the story goes, accepted a dare to mount an unbroken colt that no one had been able to ride. The instant he got in the saddle the horse reared up and whirled about, trying desperately to throw the boy.

The future president lived like an Indian during his years on the frontier. Here, he cooks his meat over a camp fire.

Young Washington and a companion pole a raft up a river.

George held the reins fast as the high-strung, nervous animal kept plunging and rearing all over the meadow. Finally, with a frenzied leap high in the air, the colt broke a blood vessel and fell down dead. It was only then that George left the saddle.

During the years that he spent on the frontier as a boy surveyor, he lived like an Indian. He slept on the ground in his clothes, and cooked his meat on forked sticks. He trudged miles every day through the roughest kind of terrain, and his body became lean and tough.

The frontier that George knew was the "Wild West" of that time. It was his training school. Presidents Andrew Jackson, Abraham Lincoln, and Theodore Roosevelt were to attend the same school. They, too, knew the frontier, but Washington was its first graduate.

When he grew to manhood he stood six feet, three inches in his stockings and weighed about 190 pounds. Most college athletes today are at least six feet tall, but in Washington's time the average man was two or three inches shorter than he is now. George was huge for his day, a giant among his fellow men. Broad-shouldered and trim-waisted, with big hands and feet (he wore size thirteen

11

boots), he stood as straight as an Indian and there was no fat on him.

As a young man he did not look anything like the portraits we usually see of him, especially the popular one by painter Gilbert Stuart, which is on the dollar bill. This shows the dignified, almost stone-faced Washington of later life when he wore ruffled lace and a well-groomed white wig.

The younger Washington had reddish-brown hair which was drawn tight and knotted in back. His face was scarred and pitted by smallpox and his eyes were blue and penetrating, like cold steel.

"He was not what the ladies would call a pretty man," one of his officers recalled, but he was not ugly. He was, in fact, rather handsome in a rugged way. Gilbert Stuart, before whom Washington sat for hours while his portrait was being painted, studied his face and saw a hot temper smoldering beneath the calm features. "Had he been born in the forest," said the painter, "he would have been the fiercest man among the savages."

Had he been born in this century, he would surely have gone in for college athletics and would probably have been a standout. He had all the qualities that make a good team player. He was big and strong and he could move fast. He was graceful, yet he was tough and could take physical punishment. He had the will to win and would never accept defeat in anything.

It is not difficult to see the big Virginian on the football field as an end or a tackle, charging in fast and breaking up plays, or going downfield and snaring a forward pass in his big hands. In baseball he would have been the catcher — the solid backstop, steadying the pitcher, calling the right signals, and rifling a throw to second base.

He did have a good arm. The story about his throwing a silver dollar across the Rappahannock River with thirty yards to spare on the other side may well be true, although some historians say that what he really tossed was a piece of slate about the size of a silver dollar and not the coin itself. It matters little. Whatever he threw, it went farther than anything anyone else could throw from the riverbank.

When Washington was alive there were very few sports in the thirteen colonies. The popular games and sports that we know today

George Washington, the boy surveyor, in the wilds of Virginia.

did not exist then. There was no baseball, football, basketball, tennis, golf, or hockey. There were no track and field meets, no swimming meets, skiing, or crew races. The modern Olympic Games were unknown. They were not held until almost 100 years after Washington died.

There was only a handful of colleges in the country — Harvard, Yale, William and Mary College in Virginia, and a few others. At these there were no athletic teams or sports, at least no organized sports.

The term "organized sports" should be made clear here, for it will be used many times in this book. It means regulated sports, or those that are controlled by rules, which are played the same way everywhere with the same kind of equipment. Furthermore, they are governed by a group of persons who work together as an organization for the good of the sport they represent.

These groups have many different titles, but they are usually known as an association, a union, or perhaps a league. Thus, we have the National Basketball Association, the American Athletic Union, the National Football League, and so on. These sports organizations make their own rules and they decide which athletes or teams are the champions. They punish wrong-doers who harm the sport and they award medals and trophies to winning performers and teams. They do many other things, such as making schedules for teams to play, running tournaments, and keeping records. Today almost every sport is organized, whether it is amateur or professional. Even the little-known sports, such as curling, lawn bowls, and volleyball, are regulated and governed by associations. A well-known sport for youngsters that is highly organized is Little League baseball.

In colonial America many kinds of games were played but they were pick-up affairs. Schoolboys and college students would make up teams on the spot by choosing sides, just as boys do today when they meet on a playing field, "looking for a game."

Among the popular games in colonial times were cricket, stoolball, and rounders. These were bat and ball games and all three were like baseball in many respects. In each game there was a batter who tried to hit a pitched ball. If he hit it, he ran to a base. He was out if the ball was caught on the fly.

14

Cock-fighting was one of the most popular sports in colonial America.

These games were played much more frequently in the northern colonies than in the southern ones. In the north there were many more people and they lived more closely together in towns and cities. There were more schools, and therefore there was more opportunity for boys and youths to get together and play games.

In the south the population was thin. It was spread out over a large area and the plantations and farms were widely separated. There were few towns and hardly any schools. Southern boys did not often gather in large numbers as was the custom in New England, where boys would meet in schoolyards or on village greens to play games. As a result, team games were almost unknown in the south.

In Virginia and in a great part of the south, much of the land was divided into large plantations. These were enormous estates, consisting of vast forests, meadows, streams, lakes and ponds, and cultivated farmlands.

A plantation was in many ways a little kingdom in itself. At its head was the planter who lived with his family in a large, stately mansion. Negro slaves served him in the manor house and they did all the work in the fields. The planter was an aristocrat, or at least he lived like one.

Plantation life, which was the kind that George Washington knew, was easy-going and leisurely. The climate was warm, the soil was good, and the labor was done by slaves.

Thus, the wealthy planters had lots of time for sports and they went in for them on a grand scale. The most popular sports in Virginia were the same that found favor with the nobility in England at that time. They were horse racing, fox hunting, and the fighting of game cocks.

Washington was an enthusiastic follower of these sports. He attended cock fights and, like most Virginia squires, he bred and raised race horses and bet on them. He often went to the races at Annapolis, Maryland. On one trip he lost about $75 at the race track. He often won, too, but whenever he was beaten he was always prompt to congratulate a rival owner upon his "success on the turf."

Many northerners who visited the plantations could not understand how the Virginians could devote so much time to sport, especially cock fighting and horse racing. It seemed to the Yankees that the southerners did not have time for anything else.

"The Planters don't much admire Labour or any other . . . exercise except Horse racing, nor diversion, except Cock-Fighting, in which some greatly delight," wrote a northern visitor in 1724. A historian named Sydney G. Fisher agreed with this opinion. He said that the Virginians were "a race of sportsmen, cock-fighters and fox-hunters."

It used to be said of Virginians that they liked horses so much they would ride five miles to catch a horse in order to ride him one mile to church. It was a pleasant joke but there was some truth in it.

Most planters, however, did not neglect their estates for the sake of sport. Washington worked hard at managing his plantation and the more than 300 slaves he owned at one time. He ran things well, but at the same time he loved sport. He loved horses above everything else.

His career as a planter really began in 1759 when he married Martha Custis, a wealthy young widow, and settled down on his

Mount Vernon estates to enjoy the leisurely life of a Virginia squire. He was then twenty-seven years old.

Nearby lived Lord Thomas Fairfax, an English-born nobleman who had come to Virginia several years before and had established a great plantation called Belvoir. He also owned vast forest lands in the western part of the colony. It was Lord Fairfax who had employed young George to survey his lands in the wilderness.

The British nobleman had been an active sportsman in England. He liked fox hunting above everything. After he settled down in Belvoir he sent to England for his horses and foxhounds so that he could take up the sport in his new home. Soon he was riding to hounds in earnest. Sometimes he would encounter the young squire of Mount Vernon as he rode through the woods and he would invite his neighbor to join him in the chase.

Lord Fairfax taught the younger man all he knew about the sport and it was not long before Washington took it up himself on his own plantation. In time, as other planters in the surrounding country began riding to hounds, Mount Vernon became the most popular

Washington with hat off points the way to Lord Fairfax on a foxhunt in Virginia.

17

General Washington with his friends after a day's hunt.

gathering place of the aristocratic fox-hunting set of Virginia and Maryland.

During the fox-hunting season, which lasted from November to March, the great house on the banks of the Potomac River was crowded with guests and Washington spent whatever time he could spare following the hounds.

He was an ardent and superb horseman. Thomas Jefferson, himself an accomplished rider, said of Washington: "He is the best horseman of the age and the most graceful."

"Washington," wrote George W. Parke Custis, who was the great man's stepgrandson, "always superbly mounted, in true sporting costume of blue coat, scarlet waistcoat, buckskin breeches, velvet cap, and whip with long thong, took the field at day's dawn, with his huntsman Will Lee, his friends and neighbors. He rode, as he did everything, with ease, elegance and with power . . . and ridiculed the idea of its being even possible that he should be unhorsed, providing that the animal kept on its legs. The General usually rode, in the chase, a horse called Blueskin, of a dark, iron-gray color."

It was the custom at Mount Vernon to hunt three times a week. The guests were roused from their beds before daylight and breakfast was served by candlelight. They usually had corncakes and milk for breakfast. The hunt began at dawn and often lasted for hours, sometimes until three o'clock in the afternoon, when dinner was served at the main house.

The traditional sport of fox hunting, English style, has not changed since Washington's time. Its chief appeal is in the pursuit of the fox and the horsemanship involved — the hard riding, the jumps over fences and walls and across ditches and streams. It does not matter very much to fox hunters if the fox is not caught. The chase is the main thing, but if the fox is caught it is killed by the hounds.

Describing the hunt at Mount Vernon, Custis wrote: "There were roads cut through the woods in various directions, by which the aged or timid hunters, and ladies, could enjoy the exhilarating cry, without the risk of life or limb, but Washington rode gaily up to his hounds, through all the difficulties and dangers on the grounds on which he hunted . . . always in at the death, and yielding to no man the honor of the brush." (The brush is the tail of the fox. It is customarily awarded to the one who is first in at the kill.)

Many of Washington's hunts were not planned. Often he would be riding out alone on an inspection tour of his lands in company with his hounds. Sweetlips, June, Trueman, Musick, and Duchess were the names of some of his hounds. They would sometimes scent a fox and take up the chase. Washington would forget what he had set out to do and would follow them. On these solitary hunts the fox would escape more often than not.

Washington was the most enthusiastic fox hunter of his day and he devoted more time to the sport than any president who came after him. He kept track of the number of times he went fox hunting and wrote down what happened almost every time he went out. His records show that his most active year was 1768, when he was thirty-six years old. That year he took the field forty-eight times and killed eighteen foxes. Once he hunted five days in a row and once eighteen times in two months. From his first recorded hunt on January 1, 1768, until the Revolution called him in 1775, he followed the hounds 173 times and was in at more than 65 kills.

It was the gray fox of the south that Washington hunted, not the longer-running red fox of the north and of England. The southern gray fox is a tree-climber, and often when Washington's hounds were about to catch one, it would scurry up a tree and stay there. The hounds could not reach it, of course, and it was sometimes shaken down.

A chase — and there might be two or three in one day — would last anywhere from a few minutes to several hours. Washington recorded a short chase as follows: "Went a Huntg and killed a Fox, after treeing him in 35 mins. . . ."

In another part of his journal he wrote: "Went a hunting after breakfast and found a Fox at Muddy Hole and killed her . . . after a chace* of better than two hours, and treeing her twice, the last of which times she fell dead out of the Tree."

"Fishing for sturgeon but catched none," wrote George in his journal. On another page he wrote as follows: "Went a ducking between breakfast and dinner and killed a Mallard and 5 bald faces. In the afternoon went to the Ck. after Blew Wings. Killd 7 or 8."

In 1770 Washington looked longingly toward the west and decided to make another trip out there. He was thirty-eight and he wanted to see once more the great wilderness he had first seen when he was sixteen. Perhaps he felt that this would be his last trip into wild Indian country.

On October 6, 1770, he started west on horseback with his old friend, Dr. James Craik. After several days in the saddle the men reached Fort Pitt, then a rough settlement of log houses. It is now the city of Pittsburgh.

Much as he liked fox hunting, Washington found time to fish in the Potomac and he often went gunning on it for wildfowl. He fished with both line and net for sturgeon, sheepshead, and shad.

---

* Washington misspelled the word "chase" here, as he did many other words. He was a poor speller. He left school at the age of fifteen and spelled almost entirely by ear. His grammar was often poor, too. For example, he wrote in his journal: "went a hunting (after fox) and catched none." Washington was first in most things, but not in spelling and grammar.

Washington's happiest days were spent at Mount Vernon with his family.

From there, with an Indian guide named the Pheasant and an interpreter, they canoed up the Monongahela River toward the Ohio country. Soon the four men were beyond the reaches of civilization.

One day they came across a war party of sixty Indians of the Six Nations tribes from the New York region who were on their way to attack the Catawbas down in the Carolinas. Fortunately, the painted braves were so anxious to battle their Indian enemies that they paid no attention to the Washington party.

On the first of November the men started up the Kanawha River in what is now West Virginia. They traveled for two days and then made camp and decided to go on a hunt. Wild game was everywhere in those days and there were no laws to limit the number of animals a hunter could kill. Washington and Dr. Craik killed five buffalo and three deer.

Washington returned to Mount Vernon on December 1, having been absent from it nine weeks and one day. For the next five years he enjoyed the life of a Virginia planter. It lasted until 1775, when he was given command of the Continental Army and went off to war.

He did not return to live at Mount Vernon again for eight years. His kennels and stables fell off badly during the Revolution, but he rebuilt them and in 1785 once more took up the chase.

He was then in his fifties and had taken on a little weight, but he still stood straight and he was as graceful as ever in the saddle. However, he was not as active as he had been before the Revolution.

During this period of his Mount Vernon residence (from 1783 to 1789) he hunted only twenty-three times and killed less than ten foxes. His final hunt at Mount Vernon took place on February 15, 1788, a week before his fifty-sixth birthday. Of this hunt he wrote: "Let out a fox [which had been taken alive a few days before] and after chasing it an hour lost it."

The next year he was made president and moved to New York City, which was then the capital of the United States. Again he was absent from Mount Vernon for a period of eight years. He did not come home until his retirement from the presidency in 1797, when he was sixty-five years old.

He was too old to run with the hounds but, as he had always done before, he mounted a horse every day and rode out to inspect his lands. No longer was he the dashing horseman in scarlet waistcoat and velvet cap. He wore somber clothes and rode alone.

A description of him in his final days has been handed down to us by Custis, his stepgrandson. An old soldier named Richard Meade, who had known Washington during the Revolution, came to Mount Vernon to pay his respects to his former commander. He rode up to the big house and asked Custis where he could find General Washington. Custis told him which way to go and added: "You will meet, sir, with an old gentleman, riding alone in plain dark clothes, a broad-brimmed white hat, a hickory switch in his hand, an umbrella with a long staff which is attached to his saddle-bow; that personage, sir, is General Washington."

So rode the first of the sporting presidents in the last two years of his life. December 12, 1799, was his last day on a horse. Two days later he died in bed of a throat infection.

CHAPTER 2

The New England Scene

JOHN ADAMS, our second president, was a chubby little man who thought that most games and amusements were a waste of time. A Puritan at heart, he frowned upon "idle diversions."

"Let others waste their bloom of life at the card or billiard table among rakes and fools," wrote John Adams, the serious-minded and very proper New Englander. As for such frivolities as dancing, he threw up his hands in horror at the thought. "I never knew a dancer who was good for anything else," he snorted.

The first two presidents were as far apart in their attitude toward recreation as it is possible for two men to be. Washington liked almost everything that Adams disliked in the way of games and sports, indoors or outdoors.

Washington loved to play cards and often gambled with his friends for small stakes. He spent hours at the billiard table and especially enjoyed playing with Lafayette, who introduced the French method of play to America. Washington was an enthusiastic and nimble-footed dancer. (He danced two cotillions and a minuet at his inaugural ball in 1789.)

John Adams did not disapprove of sports when he was a boy, nor when he was a student at Harvard College. In later life, however, he looked upon such activities with a critical eye.

Although he was never an athlete nor a sports-loving president, he is included in this book because he was a typical New England boy who took part in the games and recreations of his time — as a lad on his father's farm and as a college student.

His life from infancy has been recorded by historians and thus, through him, we are able to observe the daily life of an average youth in a northern colony 200 years ago. We know the kind of games that were played in those days and what it was like to grow up in a New England town with the sea at the front door and the wilderness just around the next bend in the road.

It was a harder life than the one young Washington knew on the plantation, but it was not "all work and no play" in New England. True, work came first because there was a greater need for it in the north. The winters were long and harsh, the rocky soil yielded fewer crops, and the threat of starvation was a reality. The early settlers well knew that they had to work hard to keep alive, so they passed laws against idleness.

Indeed, the very first game ever played by white men in New England was broken up by the Governor of Plymouth Colony, William Bradford. It happened on Christmas Day, 1621, scarcely a year after the *Mayflower* had landed at Plymouth.

On that day Governor Bradford called the Pilgrims to work, but a group of thirty-five newcomers from England asked to be excused. They said that it went against their conscience to work on Christmas Day. The Governor, a reasonable man, said that if that were so then they did not have to work. And so, off to work went the Governor with the other Pilgrims.

When he came home for his midday meal at noon he was astonished to find the men of conscience playing games. They were (as he later wrote): "In ye street at play, openly; some pitching ye barr, & some at stoole-ball, and shuch like sports."*

This was a little too much for the Governor. Quickly he stepped among the players and "tooke away their implements." He told

* Pitching the bar was throwing a crowbar for distance. Stoolball was a primitive form of cricket. A three-legged stool was upended and a batter stood before it, either bare-handed or with a bat. A ball was pitched to him and he tried to keep it from hitting the stool. If it did, he was out. He was also out if he hit the ball and it was caught on the fly. The winner was the player making the most hits. Sometimes two stool were used. Then the batter would run from one to the other when he hit the ball, thus scoring runs.

24

John Adams, our second president, played "bat and ball" and many oher games in his boyhood.

them that it was against *his* conscience "that they should play & others worke" and that "ther should be no gameing or revelling in ye streets." That was the end of the game.

Ten years before this happened a similar event had taken place in the Jamestown Colony in Virginia, where the settlers were dying of disease and starvation.

In May, 1611, Sir Thomas Dale, who was in command of a relief ship sent from England to save the starving colonists, came ashore at Jamestown and the first thing he saw was a group of men bowling in the streets. The sight of these players, who should have been working, made Sir Thomas so angry that he stopped the game and threatened to put them in irons. Thus ended the very first game recorded in America's history of sports.

In the beginning both Virginia and New England passed laws against amusements and idleness. In a few years Virginia's laws became more lenient, but things moved more slowly in New England. There were two main reasons for this.

One, as we have seen, was the harder struggle to survive, which made work a necessity. The other reason was the great number of Puritans who settled in New England.

These people were the great disapprovers in colonial America. They were suspicious of, if not downright hostile toward, almost everything that gave pleasure to anyone. The strictest among them believed that amusements in any form were invented by the devil.

They passed laws against dice playing, card playing, quoits, lawn bowling, ninepins, and shuffleboard (a tavern game played on a table with disks which were pushed by hand). Of course, they would not allow dancing.

However, it must not be assumed that all the New England pioneers were solemn and gloomy, and dedicated to day-long labor without any recreation. There were many who liked sports and gaiety, who wore bright clothes and knew how to smile, among the thousands who came to Massachusetts a few years after the landing

The Puritans of New England disapproved of sports. This picture served as a warning to those who played games on Sunday.

Severall young men playing at foote-ball on the Ice upon the LORDS-*DAY are all Drownd*

of the Pilgrims. In one ten-year period (1630-1640) about 16,000 persons sailed across the Atlantic Ocean and joined the Massachusetts Bay Colony. Of this number only 4,000 were church members.

They kept on coming. They brought with them, among other things, the Englishman's love of sports and games. Gradually, as more and more colonists arrived, New England's attitude toward sports became more liberal. By the time John Adams was born, the colony was no longer as rigidly controlled by the Puritans as it had been. Still, he was influenced by Puritanism all his days, as evidenced by his utterances against gaming and dancing.

The oldest in a family of three boys, John was born on his father's farm in 1735, three years after the birth of George Washington. The farm was in the town of Braintree (the part that is now Quincy) about ten miles south of Boston and only a mile from the sea.

The small plain farmhouse in which he was born was built in 1675. It has been standing in the same place ever since. It is now a museum and open to the public. Visitors wandering through it often comment on the narrow doorways and how low they are. A six-footer passing from one room to another has to bend his head a little lest he scrape it against the top of the doorway. This is further proof that the men and women of 200 years ago were shorter than they are now.

John Adams never had any trouble walking through those doorways. He was five feet, seven inches tall when he was a man. As a boy he was slight of build and a little shorter than most of his playmates.

They called him Johnny and he was a slender, blue-eyed youngster with light brown hair. He was always on the go, always running even to school, which he hated.

This was Mr. Cleverley's school, and it is no wonder that he hated it. Every morning, after helping his father do the chores on the farm, he had to be in his seat at school by eight o'clock. It was a long mile from home and often he had to trudge through deep snows all the way.

From eight until five in the afternoon he sat straight upright on a hard bench with a Latin grammar at hand. He was taught nothing but Latin for about four years. Not until he was twelve did he begin to learn arithmetic.

John Adams studied Latin eight hours a day in a school like this one.

The steady pounding of Latin into his system, the discipline, and the boredom of the classroom made him long keenly for the outdoors. Like many a boy, he played hooky now and then. Often he would beg his father to let him stay home from school and work around the farm. Anything to get out of school.

Away from school, John would roam the nearby fields and woods in search of wild honey, perhaps, or to gather mushrooms and nuts, or to hunt snapping turtles. He loved to fish and he knew where the trout were in the streams and when the smelt were running in Wollaston Brook. He swam well and he was in the water most of the summer.

His uncles, who lived nearby, were great hunters and whenever they started off on a partridge-shooting expedition John would appear as if by magic and beg to be taken along. They always let him come because he knew where the partridge were feeding and he would take his uncles to the right places.

He was fond of riding and whenever he got a chance he would mount one of the farm horses and ride it bareback around the meadows. This was country-style riding. The horses were big, solid-bodied animals, a far cry from the fine saddle horses that Washington rode. Nevertheless, John learned how to ride well and this helped him a few years later when he acted as a dispatch carrier and had to ride hard and fast from one colony to another.

He was always ready for a contest of any kind. There were enough boys in the village of Braintree to make up sides, or teams, for the various kinds of games they played. What these games and pastimes were and what part John took in them are mentioned in a letter he wrote when he was an old man of seventy-eight.

In recalling his early days on the farm, the ex-president wrote of John Adams, the boy, as follows:

"When he," wrote John Adams, speaking of himself in the third person, "played Truant, and when he did not, he spent all his mornings, Noons and Nights in making and sailing Boats, in swimming, skating, flying kites and shooting, in marbles, Ninepins, Bat and Ball, Football, etc., etc., Quoits, Wrestling and sometimes Boxing, etc., etc., and what was no better, running about to Quiltings and Huskings and Frolicks and Dances among the Boys and Girls!!! These 15 years went off like a Fairy Tale."

Here we see the old man clucking at himself in mild disapproval, as shown by his phrase "and what was no better," yet at the same time remembering an active and normal boyhood with relish. He was, after all, a very ordinary boy and not unlike hundreds of other colonial boys of his day.

Most of the games and pastimes he mentions in the above paragraph explain themselves, such as quoits, skating, wrestling, and so forth. But what were quiltings and huskings? And what kind of bat and ball game did they play in those days? What was their football like?

First, the quiltings and huskings were social gatherings at which games were played but were not games in themselves.

A quilting bee, as this affair was usually called, was a get-to-gether of women for the purpose of making quilts. They brought along their children who played games of all sorts, or perhaps went coasting and skating while their mothers sewed and gossiped.

Corn-husking bees played an important part in the work of the autumn harvest. Entire families gathered for these affairs, which generally started with people sitting on the floor of a barn. The corn, newly brought in from the fields, would be stripped of its coverings, or husks, and everybody took a hand in it. Along with these all-day festivals there would be singing, dancing, feasting, and the playing of many kinds of games.

Football came into the colonies from England with the earliest settlers, and it was at least 100 years old here when John Adams first played it. The sport — and it is stretching things to call it that — was nothing like our modern college game. If anything it resembled soccer but it wasn't much like that game, either.

It consisted of a group of players kicking an air-filled bladder in a leather casing, or perhaps a roundish leather bag stuffed with rags or sawdust. The idea was to advance the ball by kicking it. The playing area could be a field, a meadow, or a street of any size or shape.

There were no written rules. Any number of players could be on a side. There were no goals, no scoring, and no time limit on the length of play. Actually, football as it was played in this country until the 1830's was not a game at all. It was merely a pastime, a pleasant recreation. It gave boys and young men a good excuse to get outdoors and have some fun and exercise by kicking a ball around.

It was popular, however, and it was played so frequently in the streets of Boston that it was considered a nuisance. The citizens of the town passed by-laws against it, the first of which appeared on the books in 1701 and read as follows:

"For preventing danger by Foot Balls, Squibs [firecrackers] and Snow-balls."

Another order passed at a later date stated: "Football, not to be played at, or kicked through any part of the town" (of Boston).

The "Bat and Ball" game that John Adams played in his youth was an early form of baseball called rounders. The same game was also known as town ball because village lads played it on the town greens of New England while their elders attended town hall meetings.

Rounders came from England and it was first played here shortly

30

Town ball, the forerunner of baseball, was a popular game in colonial New England.

after the Pilgrims landed. Although the rules varied in different colonies, the objective of the game was the same everywhere. It was to score runs by hitting a ball and running around the bases. The batter was out on balls caught on the fly. If he hit a grounder the player fielding it would throw the ball at the batter and try to hit him with it as he ran for first base. If he got hit, he was out. There were no basemen.

When there were not enough players to form two teams, then two or three players would be the batters and the rest would be the fielders. In this case the game was very similar to three-old-cat. In any event, the fundamentals of baseball, which developed from rounders, were present: the pitcher, the batter, the base hit, and the run.

The playing equipment in John Adams' day was primitive. The bat was a fence post or a stout paddle. The ball had a leather cover and was stuffed with horsehair. It was about the size of the softball in use today. Gloves and mitts were unknown.

John Adams, aged fourteen, was playing rounders one day when his father summoned him from the field and told him that he was spending too much time at bat and ball and not enough time at his

Latin. He would never get to Harvard that way, his father said.

The talk had its effect. The next year, just before his sixteenth birthday, John went to Harvard. He went reluctantly, though, for he wanted to quit school and stay in Braintree. He wished only to be a farmer and a part-time cobbler, as his father was.

He was depressed by the college rules, which he had to learn before he was admitted. The first one he saw on the list was a piece of bad news for him. Students could not keep a gun, the rule stated. This meant that for the next four years he could not roam the Cambridge countryside in search of game. He knew that the woods and marshes around Cambridge were full of partridge, woodcock, duck, rabbit, and squirrel, but he would not be allowed to shoot them.

Just as bad were some other rules: students must not fish, or "scate over deep waters." The Charles River was right at Harvard's front door. It was full of fish and covered with miles of smooth ice in winter, but there would be no fishing in it or skating on it for John Adams, Harvard student.

There were twenty-four students in his freshman class and their ages ranged from twelve to twenty-two. At that time Harvard rated a student according to the social position of his family. The higher the rating, the more the privileges for the favored students, such as a choice of the better rooms and better seats at the upper table in the dining hall. Since John came from a line of farmer folk and did not have an aristocratic ancestry, he was ranked fourteenth in his class.

John did not mind being placed in the lower half of the class. The social rating system was widespread throughout New England and was accepted by everyone. It was by no means limited to Harvard. The system grew out of the Puritans' traditional custom of seating the most prominent people in church in the front pews.

What John *did* mind were the long hours of study, the strict discipline, and the lack of freedom. He soon got used to the routine, however, and became a brilliant student. The daily program for Harvard's ninety boys was designed to keep them busy — and it certainly did. It went along these lines:

The rising bell rang at five o'clock. Prayers were held an hour later and then came breakfast. The usual fare was bread and beer. Classes started at eight and ended at noon for dinner, the heartiest meal of the day.

American college students played cricket before and after the Revolution, but the game eventually gave way to baseball. Above, a cricket game at Dartmouth College in 1793.

After dinner the students could enjoy the only recreation period of the day, which lasted until two o'clock. As a rule, John would rush from the dinner table as soon as he had eaten and go to the playing field, which was in back of the college quadrangle. There was always a game going on — of rounders or football and sometimes cricket.

The boys had to be back in their rooms at two o'clock for an afternoon of study. The supper bell rang at six and right afterward there was another study period in the rooms. Curfew sounded at nine o'clock and all candles were snuffed out. Often on winter mornings, when John got up with the rising bell to build a fire in his fireplace, he would find his inkwell frozen solid.

Harvard was already "old Harvard" in 1751 when John was a freshman, having been founded more than a century before. It had an excellent reputation and it attracted students from all over the colonies. Many southerners attended the college and most of them were sons of wealthy plantation owners.

These young men had no Puritan background and they went in

for sports and games without restraint, including cards and dice. In this they were miles apart from their New England college mates.

They were, John noted, always talking in a worldly way about cock fighting, horse racing, and other things strange to New England ears. The boys were likeable enough, to be sure, with their fine manners and graceful ways, but they gambled and they were late for morning prayers. Incidentally, they were always at the top of the social standing list, or close to it.

They must have enjoyed poking fun at their northern classmates, in answer, perhaps, to the visiting Yankees who had found the southerners to be a "race of cock-fighters and fox-hunters."

Maybe so, they may have said, but who would want to live in Boston, where the theater is forbidden and the only sports are on Training Days?*

Was it the southerners who led John to write these lines in his college notebook: "Let no trifling, or amusements, or company decoy you from your book; i.e., no girl, no guns, no cards, no flutes, no violins, no dress, no tobacco, no laziness"? Or was it his New England conscience speaking?

Whatever impelled him, John Adams established a fine record at Harvard and went on to become a lawyer, patriot, statesman, ambassador, vice-president (for eight years under Washington), and president.

The next three presidents who followed John Adams to the White House had much in common. They were born and reared in Virginia, and were plantation owners and college graduates. In the order of succession they were Thomas Jefferson, James Madison, and James Monroe.

Of them Jefferson was perhaps the most athletic. He began to ride at the age of two and he was an accomplished horseman during his long life of eighty-three years. (He died on July 4, 1826, on which day John Adams, aged ninety, also died.)

Jefferson enjoyed fishing and hunting, but he was never the enthusiast that his friend, George Washington, was. Once, however, the two men went together on a fishing expedition at sea.

---

* A New England Training Day was the periodic mustering of all able-bodied men of a town for military drill, for which they gathered on the town common, or green. Afterward they engaged in sports that generally included target shooting for prizes, foot racing, wrestling, and jumping contests.

Caricature of a typical New England Training Day.

When Jefferson was ten years old, according to a family legend, his father gave him a gun and told him to go out into the woods alone to develop his self-reliance. The boy found no game, although he searched a long time. Finally, he came across a wild turkey that was trapped in a pen. Tying it to a tree with his garter, the lad shot it, then tossed it over his shoulder, and hauled it home to loud cheers.

He grew up to be a lanky redhead with a face full of freckles. His nickname was Long Tom when in 1760 he went to William and Mary College in Williamsburg, Virginia, at the age of seventeen.

The Virginians who went to that college were chiefly sons of plantation owners who were proud of their ancestors and their land. They liked to consider themselves aristocrats, whether they were or not. Most of the students took slaves to college with them along with their horses. This made life much easier at William and Mary than it was at Harvard.

At college Long Tom Jefferson walked and ran for exercise and sometimes went swimming. He was a good swimmer, as proven by the fact that he once swam back and forth across a millpond thirteen times. It was about a quarter of a mile wide.

Jefferson was one of our tallest presidents. He stood six feet, two and a quarter inches, and he must have towered over his successor, James Madison, at the latter's inauguration. For Madison was the shortest and slightest president of all.

John Quincy Adams as a young boy.

He measured only five feet, four inches, and weighed about 100 pounds. He was shy and retiring, too frail for active sports, but he loved nature and was an eager bird-watcher. Madison went to Princeton and graduated in 1771.

The little man was sandwiched in between two tall presidents. His successor, James Monroe, was the third consecutive Virginian to occupy the White House, and stood an even six feet. A vigorous, broad-shouldered youth, he liked to fish and hunt in the woods of Westmoreland County, where his father owned a large tract of land. He did not have much time for these sports, however, as he entered William and Mary at sixteen and left two years later to fight the British. He took part in several battles before receiving a bad shoulder wound which sidelined him from the Revolution and from sports.

Twenty-four years after John Adams vacated the White House, his son, John Quincy Adams, moved in. Physically, our sixth president was very much like his father, being bald, short (five feet, seven), and chubby. The two had many other things in common.

They were born in farmhouses standing next to each other on the same plot of land and were rocked in the same cradle. Both went to Harvard, became lawyers, served as ministers to Holland and England, and were presidents of the United States for a single term.

Both had rather chilly personalities, caring little for the company or the opinion of others, and both did considerable hand-wringing, New England style, in their diaries about indolence and the waste of time. This is what the hard-working John Quincy Adams wrote in his diary when he was a young man:

"I go but little into company and yet I am not industrious. Indolence, Indolence, I fear, will be my ruin."

Quincy did not have much of a boyhood if sports and games are a measure. He grew up during the Revolution when almost all the schools in the young nation were closed. The Continental Congress, which made the laws of the thirteen colonies, spoke out against amusements in any form as the Revolution got under way. One of its articles requested the colonies to "discourage every species of extravagance and dissipation, especially all horse racing and all kinds of gaming, cock fighting, exhibits of shows, plays . . . and other diversions."

If young Quincy couldn't play games, he could at least ride a horse and he must have been good at it. When he was only nine years old he was made mail-carrier between the village of Quincy and Boston. The round-trip distance was more than twenty miles, but the undersized youngster rode the route every day with a mail-bag in front of him slung across his saddle. He did this for two years.

At eleven he went abroad with his father to help him in his ministerial duties. He stayed in Europe for five years, and when he returned he spoke several languages and was a polished, educated young man. His experiences abroad gave him a more tolerant view of sports, sometimes to the chagrin of his less urbane American friends.

One of the first things he did when he became president was to install a billiard table in the White House. He had learned the game in Europe and he saw no harm in having a round or two now and then. However, the protests were loud when people heard about it, especially because he billed the government for the equipment, as follows: "billiard table $50; cues $5; billiard balls $6." He was denounced as a spendthrift. Eventually, he paid the government back out of his own pocket.

In the White House, John Quincy Adams led a Spartan existence. He would rise between four and five o'clock every morning and go outdoors as soon as he dressed, without bothering about breakfast.

President Adams' clothes were stolen while he splashed about in the Potomac river.

It was his custom to go for a walk of about five miles. Sometimes he would mount one of the horses stabled in the White House barn and ride ten or fifteen miles.

One of his favorite sports was swimming. The Potomac River is but a short walk from the White House grounds and on summer mornings the President would slip down to the river bank, undress, and plunge in.

He was an excellent swimmer. Early morning visitors to Washington would sometimes see the rotund President sporting about in the water. When he emerged he would put on his clothes and amble back to his study to read the Bible and the daily newspapers before his breakfast at nine o'clock.

One time, according to an oft-repeated story, he had his clothes stolen while he was swimming. When he emerged from the water he hid himself in a clump of bushes until a stroller passed by. The President explained his plight and asked the man to go to the White House and get some clothes for him.

This did not stop the President from taking his morning swims. He continued to enjoy them — but no doubt with a more watchful eye on his clothes. In later life he attended a Boston swimming school and used to dive off a six-foot-high springboard.

CHAPTER 3

The Frontier Presidents

THERE WAS NO love lost between John Quincy Adams and his successor, Andrew Jackson. Adams said that Jackson was "a barbarian who could not write a sentence of grammar and hardly could spell his own name."

This was an exaggeration, but it is true that Andrew Jackson was a poorly educated backwoodsman totally unlike the suave and cultured Adams. Andy, as he was called in his youth, was a true son of the frontier. He was the first president born in a log cabin and the first who was not of the Virginia aristocracy or a Massachusetts Adams.

Andy came into the world fatherless. Two weeks before he was born in a shack in the North Carolina forest, his pioneer father died and was buried in an unmarked grave. Andy grew up wild in a rough and distant country. He went to a log-cabin school and learned to read and write, but his heart was not in the classroom. It was in the enormous outdoors, where he could fish and hunt and ride his shaggy horse at full gallop over mountain trails.

Like all frontier boys, he had his own musket from the time he was strong enough to pick one up. He was a crack shot, too. John Quincy Adams used to say of himself that he could not remember when he was unable to read. Andy might have said that he could not remember when he was unable to shoot a musket or ride a horse.

He was a nimble, long-legged youth with a crest of red hair and a temper to match it. He was tall for his age but not awkward and he was fast afoot. Not many could beat him in a foot race or at broad jumping.

At fourteen John Adams had mastered Latin and was about to enter Harvard. His son at that age was secretary of the American Legation in Russia and spoke three languages fluently.

Andy Jackson at fourteen was engaged in less cultural pursuits. He wrote in his school notebook these instructions to himself: "How to feed a Cock before you him fight. Take and give him some Pickle Beaf Cut fine." (As a speller he was no better than George Washington.)

He was still in his early teens when he lost his mother and his two brothers and was left alone in the world without a penny. But he was so tall and strong that he could pass for at least eighteen. A recruiting sergeant accepted him as a volunteer in the Revolutionary Army.

Andy dashed about on his horse carrying messages through the lines and, as he said of the British, "popping them" with his musket. He was captured and scarred for life by the sword of a British officer whose boots he refused to clean. In prison he almost died from an attack of smallpox.

When the Revolution ended, he received a small inheritance from his grandfather's estate in Ireland. With no one to guide him, the wild youth got rid of the money as fast as he could, by gambling on cock fights and horse races.

An early biography describes him when he was eighteen and living in Salisbury, North Carolina, as ". . . the most roaring, rollicking, game-cocking, horse-racing, card-playing, mischievous fellow that ever lived in Salisbury . . . the head of the rowdies hereabouts."

For all his wildness, there was nothing evil or mean about him. He did not steal, lie, or cheat, and he was not a bully. He was simply full of life and reckless, like many a frontier youth in those rough-and-ready days.

Andy hit bottom when he discovered one day in Charleston that he had spent his legacy and owed a bill for his board and lodging. In desperation, he staked his horse against $200 in a dice game.

Recalling the experience in later years, he said, "If a loser in the game, I would give the landlord my saddle and bridle, as far as they would go towards the payment of the bill, ask a credit for the balance, and walk away from the city."

Fortunately, however, the dice came up in his favor and he was able to pay his bill in full and ride out of the city. "From that moment to the present time," he said, "I have never thrown dice for a wager."

The game seemed to be a turning point in his life. Shortly afterward he decided to study law, and at the age of twenty he passed the bar examinations. His spectacular career had begun.

The slim young lawyer, who stood an inch over six feet and scaled less than 150 pounds, migrated to Nashville in the new Western District of Tennessee. He took on a man's job as Public Prosecutor. He was the only lawyer in that raw and rough country.

Frontier sports prevailed there as they did throughout the American west of the 1780's. This vast territory was the land beyond the Allegheny Mountains — the Ohio country, Illinois, Indiana, Kentucky, Tennessee. It was the land that produced Abraham Lincoln a few years later. The sports he took part in were the same kind that Jackson knew.

They differed from the eastern brand in many respects. In the west, physical strength and man-to-man contests were stressed rather than team play. The more popular sports along the frontier wherever young men gathered were wrestling,* flinging the rail (like the javelin throw but with a much heavier implement), foot racing, weight lifting, broad jumping, hurling the tomahawk (for accuracy rather than distance), and throwing the long bullet.

The long bullet was an iron ball of several pounds weight. It was thrown from a leather sling and made to roll along the ground through a marked goal. Andrew Jackson was topnotch at this sport. He was not a good wrestler, however, as he was too light and did not have the strength to cope with his opponents, who usually were heavier and more powerful.

---

* In the wrestling of those days a contestant was declared the winner if he threw his opponent to the ground without going down himself. He did not have to pin his opponent's shoulders to the ground to gain a victory.

A rifle frolic, or shooting match, on the frontier.

Perhaps the most widespread sport on the frontier, where the gun was the staff of life, was the shooting match or, as it was sometimes called, the rifle frolic. These affairs took place, as a rule, in the vicinity of a tavern. The marksmen would shoot at a small target or a tethered turkey at distances of up to 300 yards. In colonial times the target was often a caricature drawn on a board of King George III, the despised British monarch.

The crack shots used the famous Pennsylvania rifle, which was the firearm that Daniel Boone and other pioneers carried west with them. It was also known as the Kentucky long rifle, but it originated in Pennsylvania. A typical rifle weighed about eight pounds and was almost five feet in length. Its .45 caliber ball could kill a man at 300 yards.

Frontier marksmen performed unbelievable feats with this superb hand-made rifle. They could shoot wild turkeys in the head, drive a nail straight into a tree with a rifle ball, or split a ball into two equal pieces on a knife blade.

A popular stunt among riflemen was known as "barking a squirrel." This difficult feat was performed by killing a squirrel without hitting it with a ball. To do this the marksman had to shoot so close to the squirrel's head that the flying chips of bark would kill it. This meant perfect marksmanship, for the squirrel was generally high in the treetops and moving.

Andrew Jackson attended these rifle frolics, and although he was a good shot he did not compare with the wizards of the frontier whose very existence depended upon their shooting ability.

As he grew older and became a successful lawyer and wealthy cotton planter, he continued to train and fight game cocks. Even when he was Justice of the Tennessee Supreme Court and his hair was white, he could not resist the lure of the cockpit. Sometimes he would fight his cocks in the shadow of the courthouse where he had just presided.

His chief interest in sports, however, was horse racing and it remained so as long as he lived. At one time he had sixteen race horses in training on his plantation near Nashville, which was called the Hermitage. It was, incidentally, one of the finest estates in America and it ranks high today among our most beautiful national shrines.

General Andrew Jackson, sportsman, duelist, frontiersman, and President.

Of the many horses that Jackson owned and trained, his favorite was Truxton, a big bay stallion. He bought Truxton for $1,170 shortly after the stallion's defeat in 1805 by a horse named Greyhound. Although Greyhound had never been defeated, Jackson was convinced that if Truxton were properly trained he could beat Greyhound in a return race.

The terms of the match called for a side bet of $5,000. Jackson, who was then a general of the Tennessee militia, vigorously threw himself into training his thoroughbred. His training methods were severe. He pushed Truxton to the limit of endurance but he got the horse into razor-sharp condition.

Interest in the race was so high that people were literally betting their shirts. Jackson accepted wagers of $1,500 in "wearing apparel," which included some shirts. One of his friends put up cash, fifteen horses with saddles on their backs, and some land.

Jackson himself risked almost everything he owned except the Hermitage. Fortunately for him, Truxton beat Greyhound easily and the General's reputation as the outstanding turfman in the west was firmly established. He immediately bought Greyhound and added him to his growing stable at Clover Bottom, a race track that he partly owned.

Truxton won many more races wearing Jackson's colors. The greatest was against Ploughboy, owned by Captain Joseph Erwin of Nashville. The rivalry between these stables grew so heated that a duel was fought to settle the matter.

The horses had been matched once before but they did not meet. Erwin had called off the race and paid the forfeit under the terms of the agreement between the owners.

When the race was finally held, a Nashville newspaper announced it as follows: "On Thursday [April 3, 1806] will be run the greatest and most interesting race ever run in the Western country, between Gen. Jackson's horse TRUXTON, 6 years old carrying 124 pounds, and Capt. Joseph Erwin's horse PLOUGHBOY, 8 years old carrying 130 pounds . . . for the sum of 3,000 dollars."

The announcement attracted to Clover Bottom "the largest concourse of people I ever saw assembled, unless in the army," said Jackson. As was then the custom, the match was for the best two of three two-mile heats, horse against horse, winner take all.

Truxton went lame just before the race, but Jackson, despite the urging of his friends and backers, refused to ask for a postponement. The two horses were brought to the starting point and got off together at the tap of a drum.

To the astonishment of almost everyone except Jackson, Truxton took the lead from the start, held it, and won going away. But he finished so lame that it did not seem possible he could go another two-mile heat. Surprisingly, the Hermitage stallion took charge at the start just as before, and ran away from Ploughboy again, winning in three minutes and fifty-nine seconds.

However, the outcome of the race did not settle the rivalry between Jackson and Erwin, Ploughboy's owner. There had been a misunderstanding over the terms of the forfeit paid by Erwin for postponing the race. It had caused much ill feeling between the two owners. Charges flew back and forth. Erwin's cause was taken up by his son-in-law, Charles Dickinson, who was twenty-seven years old and was an expert pistol shot. Jackson was twelve years older than Dickinson and was not an especially good pistol shot for the western country.

Dickinson, having insulted Jackson on more than one occasion, was challenged to a duel by the General. Their seconds met and arranged the meeting and the terms, which, according to the duelling code then in use, were: "Distance, twenty-four feet; the parties to stand facing each other, with their pistols down perpendicularly. When they are READY, the single word FIRE! to be given; at which they are to fire as soon as they please. Should either fire before the word is given we (the seconds for both sides) pledge ourselves to shoot him down instantly."

Jackson knew that Dickinson was a snap shot, and deadly. He could rapidly put four balls into a mark twenty-four feet away that could be covered by a silver dollar. On the streets of Nashville he offered to bet anyone that he would kill Jackson with his first shot.

Jackson was well aware of his foe's superiority. He decided not to try for the first shot. He would let Dickinson fire first. He knew that Dickinson would hit him and might hurt him badly, but he was determined to take the ball and stay on his feet. Then he would aim carefully and shoot to kill, if it was the last thing he ever did.

That is exactly what happened. At the word "Fire!" Dickinson shot instantly. A puff of dust came from Jackson's coat near his heart. He was hit but he did not flinch. Slowly he raised his pistol.

"My God, have I missed him?" cried the horrified Dickinson and recoiled a step or two. One of the seconds drew his pistol and ordered Dickinson to get back on the mark.

Jackson faced his man who was now standing with his arms folded. He took careful aim and fired. Dickinson went down with a ball in his stomach. He died that night in agony.

Later, a surgeon who tried to remove the ball from Jackson's chest said that Dickinson's aim had been true but that he had misjudged the position of the General's heart because of the set of his coat. Jackson's coat hung loose on his slender frame. Did this save his life? Probably, but it is also probable that Dickinson would have died anyway.

"I would have hit him if he had shot me through the brain," said Jackson and those who knew him, believed him. No president was ever more determined than he.

He was a hard man to beat, in war or in sports. But there was

In his duel with Charles Dickinson, Jackson let his opponent fire first.
He took the ball without flinching, then aimed carefully and cut his man
down.

one horse his stable never could defeat, a mare named Maria. He almost lost a fortune backing his own horse against Maria. The mare came into prominence after Truxton's racing days were over, and she beat Truxton's son, Decatur, and every Jackson-owned or backed horse sent against her.

Many of these races took place during the War of 1812 while Jackson was fighting the British. During one military expedition in 1813 the General wrote Colonel W. R. Johnson to buy and send to the Hermitage "the best 4-mile horse in Virginia, without regard to price" (for the purpose of beating Maria). The following year, while Jackson was facing the British at Mobile, he found time to ship home two race horses.

When he moved into the White House in 1829 he brought with him a string of race horses and jockeys. The White House stables were not large enough for his prize thoroughbreds, and Jackson spent thousands of dollars rebuilding them.

Whether he was fighting the British or performing his duties as president of the United States he was always close to his racing stable and his thoroughbreds. The desire to beat Maria never left him.

When he was an old man in retirement at the Hermitage, a neighbor asked him if there was anything he had ever undertaken that he had failed to accomplish. The man who had served as justice, congressman, United States senator, governor of Florida, hero of the War of 1812, general, and president, quickly looked back upon his life and replied: "Nothing that I can remember — except Maria. I could not beat her."

The next great frontiersman to become president was Abraham Lincoln, who entered the White House twenty-four years after Jackson left it. During that time eight presidents were elected. None of these could be described as being interested in sports, although with two exceptions* all engaged in youthful sports and games in one way or another.

* James K. Polk (1795-1849) was too frail and sickly for sports. At the age of fourteen he survived a serious abdominal operation which was performed without an anesthetic.
  Millard Fillmore (1800-1874) at fourteen worked from twelve to fifteen hours a day as a wool weaver. He had no boyhood as we know it. His father forbade him to fish and hunt, saying that only Indians did such things.

Professional foot-racing attracted great crowds in pre-Civil War times.

The population of the United States surged forward between the Jackson and the Lincoln administrations, and with it came changes in the American sporting scene. One of the many developments was the rise of spectator sports. Before this time there was not much public interest in sporting events. Few people paid money to watch them. But now, almost overnight, huge crowds gathered and bought tickets to various contests and games.

The most popular spectator sport was horse racing, which drew crowds of up to 100,000 people. Professional foot racing, strange as it may seem to us today, was next in popularity. This sport would sometimes attract crowds of 25,000.

That was the estimated attendance at a ten-mile foot race that was run in New Jersey in 1844 for a purse of $700 to the winner. So dense was the crowd that a dozen men on horseback had to precede the runners to keep the track clear. (The race was won by John Barlow, an Englishman, in 54 minutes, 10 seconds.) This event was typical of the many staged at that time when professional foot racing was in vogue on both sides of the Atlantic.

49

Young Abe Lincoln reading before the fireplace in his log cabin home.

In lesser numbers crowds gathered to watch harness racing, base-ball, and rowing races. Harness racing (or trotting) had a great following throughout rural America. It produced the country's first national sports hero in Hiram Woodruff, who was a master reins-man and a constant winner. During his long career, which began in 1833 and lasted more than thirty years, his name was known all over the United States.

The beginning of organized baseball belongs to this era, although the sport did not become popular until after the Civil War. The first game of record took place at Hoboken, New Jersey, on June 19, 1846, when two nine-man teams — the Knickerbockers and the New Yorks — played a game under written rules. This was not rounders or town ball. It was baseball, played on a diamond with bases ninety feet apart, as they are today. Thirteen years later Williams and Amherst crossed bats in the first baseball game ever played between two colleges (Amherst won, 73 to 32) and the National Pastime was on its way.

This was not the first intercollegiate contest of any kind, though. That came about in the summer of 1852 when the Yale and Harvard crews rowed over a two-mile course on Lake Winnepesaukee in New Hampshire. Franklin Pierce, the Democratic candidate for the presidency, was among the thousands who saw Harvard win the race by two lengths. That fall Pierce was elected president. He succeeded Millard Fillmore and he was in turn succeeded by James Buchanan and Abraham Lincoln.

During this pre-Civil War era the rise of public interest in sports was mostly confined to the east, to the larger cities and areas of dense population. There had not yet been much change in the southern sporting scene. Out west on the other side of the Alleghenies there was still less of a change. The frontiersmen were still clearing land and fighting Indians. It is doubtful if a big raw-boned youth out in the Indiana wilderness named Abraham Lincoln knew anything about the crowds at the races back east.

There was no chance for sports in that remote country. There were no schools anywhere near Pigeon Creek, where the Lincoln family settled. There was "about one human being to each square mile," Abe later wrote. Families lived miles apart.

"It was a wild region," he recalled, "with many bears and other wild animals still in the woods, where the panther's scream filled the night with fear and bears preyed on the swine."

Almost the first thing Abe remembered was swinging an ax to help his father build a "half-faced" camp* to shelter the seven members of the family. He was seven years old and large for his age and "had an ax put into his hands at once," he wrote of himself in later years.

Abe developed into a tall and rangy boy. He was a hard worker but he was unusual in some ways. Unlike most frontier boys he did not like hunting. He liked to read instead.

Abe was only seven when he found out that he didn't like shooting very much. One day he was inside the family log cabin and he shot a wild turkey through a crack in the wall. "He has never since pulled a trigger on any larger game," Abe wrote of himself many years later.

* A three-walled shed with the fourth side entirely open to the wind, rain and snow. It was roofed with slabs and had a dirt floor. There were no windows. At the open side a log fire was kept burning night and day.

At seventeen he stood six feet, four inches, and he was tough and as lithe as a panther. He worked as a farm hand around Spencer County in Indiana and he found that he was as strong as any of the men who worked beside him. He was more powerful than most of them.

He also found that when he went against other farm youths in friendly wrestling matches he could throw them all. In the typical frontier sports such as throwing the maul (a very heavy hammer used for driving stakes), pitching the crowbar, foot racing and broad jumping, he could beat almost everyone his age and many who were older than himself.

His strength was tremendous. He amazed men with his lifting power. One time four farm workers were about to put poles under a chicken house so that they could carry it away. Abe stepped in, picked up the chicken house, and walked away with it to the place where the farmer wanted it. The men dropped their poles in astonishment.

His reputation as a wrestler followed him when the Lincolns moved to Coles County in Illinois in 1830. In neighboring Cumberland County the champion wrestler was Dan Needham. He had heard about Abe's wrestling and he said that if they ever met he would "fling him three best out of four any day."

Eventually the two came together at a house-raising* at Wabash Point. They were evenly matched, both standing six feet four. There was not much to the match. They grappled four times and each time Needham went down and under. Needham then lost his head and challenged Abe to a fist fight, but he calmed down as Lincoln good-humoredly talked him out of it. At last Dan put out his hand and grinned at Lincoln. "Well, I'll be damned," he said and there there was no more trouble.

Abe's biggest match took place a couple of years later when he was a twenty-two-year-old clerk in Denton Offut's store in New Salem, Illinois. A local tough named Jack Armstrong from Clary's Grove, just four miles away, had heard about Abe being able to

* A gathering of farm folk to help a neighbor build his house or erect its framework. In conjunction with the work, there were impromptu sports and games, feasting and dancing. This event, as well as barn-raising, was a feature of colonial America in the east. It went west with the pioneers and was observed until the end of the last century.

A typical house-raising in the days of Lincoln's youth.

outrun, outjump, outlift, and outwrestle any man in the county. Armstrong thought that he could throw Abe and he had many backers who agreed with him.

When the match was arranged and became known, people from fifty miles around gathered to see it. Bets ran high.

Armstrong was short and stocky with powerful muscles. From the start he tried to get in close where he could use his thick muscular strength but Abe held him off with his long arms. Gradually he wore Armstrong down and got him panting for breath. This angered Armstrong and he fouled Lincoln by stamping on Abe's foot with his heavy boot.

Now it was Abe's turn to be mad. Suddenly he lifted Armstrong up by the throat, shook him like a rag doll, and then crashed him to earth in a hard fall. Armstrong lay flat on his back, licked to a turn.

At this moment Armstrong's gang came for Lincoln. They were about to close in on him when Jack Armstrong broke through the mob and shook Abe's hand. He shouted to his gang that Lincoln had won fairly and added, "He's the best feller that ever broke into the settlement."

After that Abe was accepted by the tough Clarey's Grove boys. Even though he didn't drink or play cards, he was made one of them. They often called upon him to judge wrestling matches and horse races and to act as umpire at cock fights.

Years later William Herndon, who was Lincoln's law partner at one time, wrote a description of Abe umpiring a cock fight. "They formed a ring," he wrote. "The time having arrived, Lincoln with one hand on each hip and in a squatting position, cried 'Ready!' Into the ring they tossed their fowls, Bap's red rooster along with the rest. But no sooner had the little beauty discovered what was to be done than he dropped his tail and ran."

As you have already read, the ancient sport of cock fighting flourished throughout America from colonial times on. The sport was held under cover in New England, but it was conducted openly in the south and in much of the west of Lincoln's day. It is now illegal in all states, but it is still held secretly in many parts of the nation, particularly in the south.

When Lincoln was twenty-three he volunteered to fight in the war

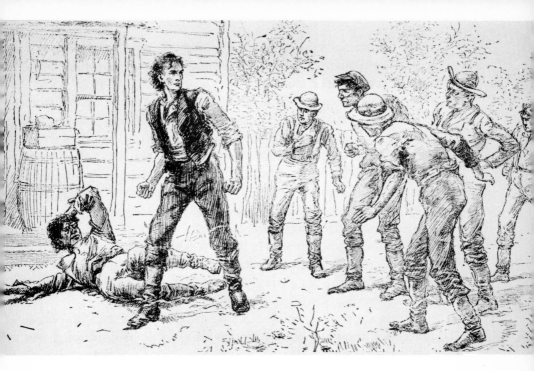

In a frontier wrestling match Abe Lincoln puts Jack Armstrong on his back, then turns to stand off the fallen man's gang.

against the Indian Chief, Black Hawk, leader of the Sac and Fox tribe. Abe was made captain of a company of Illinois volunteers. His men said that there was no one in the army that could throw their Captain Abe in a wrestling match and they had money to back him.

A soldier named Lorenzo D. Thompson dared take up the challenge, and a championship bout was arranged. Abe's supporters bet everything they had — money, knives, blankets, and tomahawks.

As the two wrestlers came together and grappled in their first feel-out of each other, Abe knew that he was in for trouble. "Boys," he said to his friends, "this is the most powerful man I ever had hold of."

Abe held his man off for awhile, until Thompson got the "crotch hoist" and down went Abe in a fair fall. The match was for the best two out of three falls. In the second grapple Abe went down again but this time he pulled Thompson with him. Both men lay on the ground.

This grapple should have been declared a draw as neither had thrown the other cleanly, but Abe raised his head and said: "Boys, give up your bets. If this man hasn't throwed me fairly, he could." Sadly, Abe's men paid off but many of them said that it should have been a draw. In any event, Abe acknowledged defeat. This was the only time he was ever beaten in a wrestling match.

It is difficult to think of Lincoln playing marbles when he became president, but he did and he excelled at the game. In those days marbles were popular with all ages. Men would play against each other, just as they might shoot a game of pool today, or go bowling.

For example, when President William Henry Harrison died in the White House on April 4, 1841, messengers were sent out on horseback to notify Vice-President John Tyler that he was now the chief executive. They found Tyler down on one knee playing marbles with his boys at his home in Williamsburg, Virginia. He didn't even know that Harrison had been ill when the messenger galloped into his yard and told him that he was the president. He did not finish out the game.

Abe used to play marbles with the New Salem youngsters in the 1830's. He kept on with the game and played it for relaxation when he got to the White House. He was an accurate shot with his taw (shooter) and he could shoot it farther than most players.

One time during the Civil War, President Lincoln was walking toward Army headquarters in Washington with a telegraph clerk and one of his sons. He picked up a small round stone from the street and challenged them to a game of shooting stones ahead for distance, marble fashion, to see who could get his stone to the Army headquarters in the least number of shots. It was Abe all the way. When they got to the steps he had won easily and had thus found in this simple game a relief from the burdens of office.

Lincoln, like Washington, was a giant and had the strength of two men. It is interesting to note that our two greatest presidents were also the tallest and the strongest.

Lincoln's first photograph, taken in 1846 when he was thirty-seven.

Ulysses S. Grant as a West Point Cadet. He was the outstanding horseman of the Corps.

CHAPTER 4

The Gas-Lit Era

HE WAS PINT-SIZED and very shy, this freckle-faced mite whose name was Hiram Ulysses Grant. He was called Ulysses, or "Lys" for short, by his parents and relatives. But most of the boys around Georgetown, Ohio, where he grew up, called him "Useless." This was because he was so small he could not hold his own in games with boys of his own age. The nickname stuck — and hurt. It changed the course of his life.

The sensitive boy became a "loner," pathetic in his hunger for the friendship of other boys but finding himself the butt of village jokes with the name of "Useless." The nickname turned him away from his schoolmates and other human beings. The companionship he sought came from horses. Among them he was at home. They gave him the feeling of power that he so badly needed.

His father owned a tannery in the village and was considered well-to-do. He allowed Lys to have a horse at a very early age. From the beginning the boy proved himself a genius at handling horses. Although he was small for his age, he had extraordinary physical strength and he made good use of it when he rode.

The following description of his amazing horsemanship in 1831, at the age of nine, was written by historian Lloyd Lewis:

"For all his sedateness and modesty, he seemed to the townsfolk to love to break fiery colts on the village square with crowds looking on. He had improvised his own technique for the struggle.

Whenever the horse suddenly stopped its plungings and reared, pawing at the sky, the little boy dug his bare heels into its flanks and hung on. When it reversed its violence . . . and flailed its hind hoofs at the treetops, he gripped its neck with his short arms and burrowed his toes in behind its shoulder blades."

He always hung on this way, refusing to quit whether it was riding a horse at nine or leading an army against the Confederacy. He became the most tenacious and successful general in the Civil War. He was "Grant, the Bulldog," who kept hammering away at the Confederacy as no other Union general did and he eventually smashed it. One wonders if this bulldog tenacity of his was not born on the village green of Georgetown, where he showed the townsfolk that he was, indeed, not "Useless."

When Lys was ten his father added a livery business to his tannery and the boy was driving passengers from Georgetown to Cincinnati, some forty-five miles distant. There was no team he couldn't manage, no horse he couldn't break.

When he wasn't driving he amused himself by riding bareback and practicing acrobatic feats on galloping horses. Whenever a circus came to town, Lys was the first to emerge from the audience at the ringmaster's challenge: "Will any boy come forth to ride this pony?"

The trick circus ponies were trained to unseat their riders with violent bucks and sudden wheelings, but they could never throw Lys. Once a ringmaster put a monkey on his shoulders to rattle him, but Lys, steady and expressionless, rode it out and kept the pony in hand.

In his *Memoirs* Grant described other childhood pleasures he found time for, such as "fishing, going to a creek a mile away to swim in summer, taking a horse and visiting my grandparents . . . fifteen miles off, skating on the ice in winter, or taking a horse and sleigh when there was snow on the ground."

Notice that he makes no mention of bat and ball games or any other team sports.

At seventeen he was given an appointment to West Point. The day before he left Georgetown a handyman in the village made a trunk for him and tacked on it Lys' initials in brass, H.U.G. Fearing that he would be ridiculed at West Point by being called "Hug," he had the tacks removed. After all, he had suffered enough with his "Useless" nickname. He decided to turn his name around to become Ulysses Hiram Grant. No one could make a nickname out of those initials.

However, when the five-foot-two-inch youth arrived at West Point in 1839 he found that he was already registered as Ulysses Simpson (his mother's maiden name) Grant, owing to an error made by the congressman who had appointed him. Rather than have the papers sent back to Washington to be changed, Lys decided right then and there to take the name of Ulysses Simpson and be done with it. And that is the famous name that has gone down in history.

At West Point his passion for horses persisted and he never lost his superb ability to handle them. The academy in those days had no organized sports; fencing and riding were about the only recreations. Grant soon became the outstanding horseman of the entire Corps, so accomplished that even the riding master was no match for him.

"It was as good as a circus to see Grant ride," a fellow cadet later recalled. "There was a dark bay horse that was so fractious it was about to be condemned. Grant selected it for his horse. He bridled, mounted and rode it every day . . . and how he did ride! He handled the refractory creature as a giant would a child. The whole class would stand around admiring his wonderful command of the beast. . . ."

Neither the class nor the faculty ever stood around admiring Grant as a student, however. He was below average in studies and conduct. In marks he stood twenty-first in a graduating class of thirty-nine, and in conduct 156 among 223 cadets in the Corps. But he could ride!

He was long remembered at the Point for the leap he made at the graduating exercises of the senior class. "The riding master placed a leaping bar higher than a man's head and called out 'Cadet Grant,' " wrote General J. B. Fry. "A clean-faced, slender, blue-eyed young fellow weighing about 120 pounds dashed from the ranks on a powerfully built chestnut sorrel horse and galloped down the opposite side of the hall. As he came into the stretch, the horse increased his pace and, measuring his stride for the great leap before him, bounded into the air and cleared the bar, carrying his rider as if man and beast had been welded together. The spectators were breathless."

Grant set the academy high-jump record which endured for twenty-five years, but the exact height is questionable. One biographer, however, has the horse clearing better than six feet.

Three years after Grant graduated from West Point, the United States and Mexico were at war. He took part in the conflict and fought in several battles. A daring ride made by the young officer at the battle of Monterey brought him further distinction as a horseman. Clinging to the side of his horse Indian-fashion, he galloped through heavy fire to reach an ammunition wagon for a fresh supply of powder and bullets. The feat made him a hero.

In Texas, where his regiment was stationed for a while, Grant discovered that he was unable to kill animals or game birds. It was then the custom for the officers to leave camp for the day to hunt deer and wild turkey for provisions. Grant could not bring himself to go with them, but one day he decided to go out alone with his gun and bring back a few turkeys.

The White House stables were enlarged during Grant's administration.

President Grant driving on Harlem Lane in New York City with his friend, Robert Bonner.

He soon saw several of the big birds. "These were followed by more," he wrote in his *Memoirs*. "I stood watching them to see where they flew — with my gun on my shoulder, and never once thought of leveling it at the birds. When I had time to reflect upon the matter, I came to the conclusion that as a sportsman I was a failure, and went back [to camp]."

After the Mexican War he was stationed at various posts and barely subsisted on his small salary. However, Grant always managed to own good trotters. One of his favorites was a little black mare he bought for $250 in Detroit, where he was stationed in 1849. Whirling behind her in a buggy, or in a cutter on the snow, he was a frequent sensation in the streets of the city. She was good enough to win a few races for him, much to his delight.

The driving of fast-stepping horses continued to be his chief relaxation after the Civil War when he lived in Washington as General of the Army and later as President. Like Jackson before him, Grant rebuilt the White House stables, and during his two terms (1869–1877) they sheltered more horses than they ever had before. He had his choice of a dozen fine horses to drive. One day, as he sped along M Street, he was arrested for fast driving. The officer, one of Washington's new Negro policemen, nearly collapsed when he saw who his prisoner was, but Grant was more amused than angered. "Officer, do your duty." He smiled and walked home while the policeman brought the horse and rig to the station house.

Another form of recreation that Grant found in the White House was the ball games played by youngsters on the grounds behind the executive mansion. Often the President would stroll over to the diamond and watch a game. Sometimes he would act as umpire or take a turn at bat.

When his tenure in the White House was over, Grant lived in New York City, and Harlem Lane (now St. Nicholas Avenue) became his favorite ground for driving fast trotters. Except for his last years, when he was confined to his home by cancer, Grant was seldom away from horses, the animals that he loved and handled so well.

In the first half of the last century interest in sports took a big jump, as we have seen, but that was nothing compared to the upsurge that swept the nation after the Civil War. This period is sometimes called the Gas-Lit era. It begins with Grant and ends with President Grover Cleveland, who left office in 1897. During this time practically all of our sports were founded and organized.

The reasons for this tremendous growth are many. Again there was a great population increase. Hundreds of thousands of immigrants poured into the United States and most of them came to the big cities. Perhaps more important, though, were the growth of industry and the development of the machine.

This meant more leisure time for everybody. The twelve-hour working day became the ten-hour day. Saturday became a half holiday. In addition, Puritanism, the great stifler of sports, was outmoded. Thus, more people had more time for sports and they no longer felt guilty about enjoying them on Sunday or any other day.

The churches no longer frowned on sports. Indeed, they encouraged them. The church gymnasium came into being at this time and the Y.M.C.A. became a leader in the promotion of sports.

In the Gas-Lit era baseball took a giant step and went professional. It became the National Pastime. Football, formerly a haphazard kicking game, grew from soccer into a distinctive American game developed by the eastern colleges. The first modern Olympic Games were held at this time, and track and field became a major college sport.

As an example of how sports organizations were developing during this period, one year, 1876, saw the formation of the National Baseball League, the Intercollegiate Football Association, and the I.C.A.A.A. (meaning the Intercollegiate Track and Field Association). The Kentucky Derby celebrated its first anniversary that year.

It was a banner year, but the list continues: Rowing Association of American Colleges (1871), the U.S. Lawn Tennis Association (1881), the American Hockey Association (1887), the U.S. Golf Association (1894), and the American Bowling Congress (1895). Basketball was invented in 1891 and soon spread to every section of the country.

There was more to come. John L. Sullivan won the bareknuckle heavyweight championship in 1882 and thereby became a national hero. He was the first sports figure to be followed on the streets by admiring crowds. (He lost the title ten years later to James J. Corbett in the first championship glove bout.) Polo, bicycle racing, trap shooting, and intercollegiate swimming began in this country at this time. Everything was happening in the field of sports.

It is difficult to think of the heavy, slow-moving man, Grover Cleveland, as a sports-loving president. He loathed exercise in every form. "Bodily movement alone . . . is among the dreary and unsatisfying things of life," said Cleveland, who weighed around 250 pounds.

Yet he was a president who loved sports, more so than most. Despite his great girth he was an active outdoorsman, a north woods camper, deer stalker, wing shot, and fresh- and salt-water fisherman. He spent so much time fishing and hunting when he was president that he was constantly criticized in the press.

"Petty forms of persecution," he snorted at his critics. "Nothing more serious than gnats suffered on the banks of a stream." He readily admitted in his book, *Fishing and Hunting Sketches*, that "as far as my attachment to outdoor sports may be considered a fault, I am . . . utterly incorrigible and shameless."

To the charge that he was "willing to associate in the field with any loafer who was the owner of a dog and gun," Cleveland admitted that it "was too nearly true to be denied."

His first remembered home was in Fayetteville, a village in central New York, where as a lad he acquired his lifelong fondness for fishing. From the pinhook and sapling stage he graduated to rod and reel, and later became a fly caster, though never a good one.

Plain Grover was no fancy angler. He was essentially a bait fisherman and he looked with suspicion upon the stream-wading purists who insisted, as he said, that "fly-casting is the only style of fishing worthy of cultivation, and that no other method ought to be undertaken by a true fisherman. This is one of the deplorable fishing affectations." He said that flycasting was "the most showy" form of fishing. He took delight in pointing out that when the trout weren't taking flies "those super-refined flycasting dictators . . . will chase grasshoppers . . . and turn over logs and stones with feverish anxiety in quest of worms."

In all matters Cleveland was plain-spoken and his tastes were simple. Nothing fancy for him. When he entered the White House in 1885 he was dismayed to find a French chef in charge of the kitchen. The chef had been hired by the previous president, Chester A. Arthur, who had entertained lavishly and lived high. Cleveland could not stand the Frenchman or his cooking.

"I must go to dinner," he once wrote a friend from the White House. "I wish it was to eat a pickled herring, Swiss cheese and a chop at Louis' instead of the French stuff I shall find."

In 1885 President Cleveland, in company with a few friends and four north woods guides, went on a camping trip in the Adirondack Mountains of New York. They disappeared into the wilderness without leaving word where they were going or when they would return. Such a presidential trip nowadays would be unthinkable; it would not be allowed. The Cleveland party lost all contact with civilization. No Secret Service men, secretaries, assistants, clerks, newspapermen, or servants went with them.

Several days later a reporter from the New York *World* went into the woods to find the "lost" President. After a hard trip he finally came across the campers and had breakfast with them. It was a Cleveland-style meal of broiled venison, baked potatoes, and hot buttered biscuits. It was served on a rough board supported by stakes. Logs were used as chairs.

The President seemed "to have gained considerable flesh since he went into the mountains," the reporter later wrote, "and his manner betokened some fatigue and lassitude. I was told by one of his guides that the arduous journey through the forest had exhausted him so much that for two days after reaching camp he had been unable to move freely about. . . . The life he is leading in his retreat in the wilderness is evidently too much for him. It is totally unadapted for any but the hardiest woodsman."

Cleveland may not have been hardy, but he was good-natured and willing. One can see the rotund, five-foot-eleven-inch President puffing up the trails like a locomotive straining to make a steep grade.

He slept with the others, including the guides, on balsam boughs spread out on the dirt floor of a low-roofed cabin. When the men went to bed they simply shed their outer clothing and wrapped themselves in blankets.

Cleveland did more fishing than hunting on the trip. Sometimes, though, he would go out with the others at night to "jack" a deer. This method of hunting is now illegal and many outdoorsmen even in Cleveland's time considered it unsportsmanlike. It consists of shining a spotlight on a deer. The strong light bewilders the animal and it stands perfectly still in its tracks, thus making it an easy shot.

It must be remembered, however, that the sportsmanship code in those days was not as rigid as it is now. Also, there were fewer fish and game laws and most of them were not seriously enforced.

In the Gas-Lit era Americans mistakenly believed that their wildlife resources were inexhaustible. Gunners shot down so many ducks that they didn't bother to count their daily bag. They fell from the skies by the millions. An estimated 15,000 ducks a day were killed on Chesapeake Bay alone in the 1870's. In the Dakota Territory, where the wild goose was shot from pits dug in wheat fields, gunners brought down so many that they barely had time to leave their pits between shots to collect the fallen birds.

In 1878 Iowa, seeking to control this senseless slaughter, became the first state to fix a bag limit on game. Today federal law protects migratory waterfowl. The daily limit is four ducks per person.

Cleveland was often bothered by rumors and false stories portraying him as a game hog and violator of the game laws. These stories, which were untrue, outraged him. "False and mischievous . . . was the charge that a party of which I was a member killed 500 ducks," he stated. He pointed out that even if it were true, it would not have been a violation of the law for five gunners to shoot 500 birds in four days. But it was not true, he insisted. "Our party killed about 125 ducks," he said.

On Chesapeake Bay and in the Carolinas, where he so often shot, he would sit in a duck blind from dawn to darkness. He scorned the customary midday return to camp and quit only when he got his limit.

He was a fine wing shot and frequently got doubles. Often he would "wipe the eye" of a shooting companion. (The sporting term "wiping the eye" means bringing down a bird with a long shot after the other had missed it.) " 'Gouging the eye' would be a more fitting term," said Cleveland, who sometimes had his own eye wiped and did not like it.

Once he tried out an enormous eight-gauge shotgun and fired both barrels. Huge as the President was, he was knocked flat in the bottom of the blind by the recoil, and he never used the gun again.

On Cape Cod, where he spent the summers of the '90's, President Cleveland fished almost daily — for bluefish and weakfish on Buzzard's Bay and for bass on the inland freshwater ponds. He fished Cape Cod streams for sea-run brook trout, which were known locally as salters.

His favorite companions were Joe Jefferson, the country's most famous actor, and Richard W. Gilder, the editor of *Century* magazine. The President, Gilder marveled, "will fish when it shines and fish when it rains; I have seen him pull bass up in a lively thunderstorm, and refuse to be driven from a Cape Cod pond by the worst hail-storm I ever witnessed or suffered. He will fish through hunger and heat, lightning and tempest."

Cleveland usually wore a flopping straw hat and an encircling kerchief which was knotted under his triple chin. He once told Gilder that when he was on the water he could cast his public cares

President Grover Cleveland
was a devoted fisherman.

aside, but that they would come crushing down upon him the moment he put foot on dry land.

He had great admiration for the smallmouth black bass. "I consider these," he said, "more uncertain, whimsical and wary in biting, and more strong, resolute and resourceful when hooked, than any other fish caught in fresh waters. They will . . . rise to a fly; but this cannot be relied upon. They can be taken by trolling; but this is very often not successful, and is at best a second-class style of fishing. On the whole it is best and most satisfactory to attempt their capture by still-fishing with bait."

Next to fishing his favorite sport was quail shooting. He would willingly tramp miles over rough terrain for quail, but the quick-rising birds whirring up in the field gave him a good deal of trouble.

"I do not assume to be competent to give instruction in quail shooting," he admitted. "I miss too often to undertake such a role." He suffered from what he called "quick triggeritis." A remedy for this common fault of shooting too soon was once given him by a veteran quail shooter: "When the bird gets up, if you chew tobacco spit over your shoulder before you shoot." He was more at home in a duck blind where he could see the birds coming in and get set for a shot.

Cleveland is the only president who served two separate terms (1885–1889 and 1893–1897). Following his second term he went into retirement at Princeton, where he became a favorite of the students. Although he never attended college, he became an avid football fan at Princeton. Two of the best seats at Brokaw Field were reserved for Cleveland and his wife. When the team won a big victory the students would celebrate by marching to Cleveland's home and demanding his appearance.

The big, jovial ex-president would always come out on the porch and say a few pleasant words to the crowd. He would lead them in the Princeton cheers and then go back into the house, perhaps to play a game of billiards — his favorite indoor sport.

For several years thereafter he went duck and quail shooting every season, fished New Hampshire's lakes and the waters of Buzzard's Bay each summer. At Princeton he roamed the field for rabbits.

"An entirely suitable member of the game community," he said of the cottontail. "I am not ashamed of their pursuit."

In his last years Cleveland's figure lost its fullness, his tread became more slow and measured and his shooting trips were postponed "until next fall." Before "next fall" came, he died at Princeton in 1908, aged seventy-one.

In the Gas-Lit era there were few game laws, and gunners shot down ducks by the millions.

CHAPTER 5

Teddy Roosevelt and His Times

IN THE FALL OF 1864, when General Grant was pounding away at the Confederates in Virginia, an undersized, sickly boy named Theodore Roosevelt celebrated his sixth birthday in New York.

He was far more concerned about his Shetland pony, called General Grant, than he was about the other Grant. In fact, he had not yet heard of him. When he did he was surprised that a man should have the same name as his pony.

One of his earliest recollections was riding General Grant. Another and less pleasant one was of his father taking him from the bed and walking the floor with him when he would awaken gasping for breath in the night. He suffered from asthma throughout his boyhood.

Worse still was another physical deficiency, but it was not discovered until he was thirteen and was given a gun by his father. This was his near-sightedness. He found out about it when he went out hunting with his companions and discovered that they could see things to shoot at that he could not see. He had no idea how poor his eyesight was until he was fitted with his first pair of spectacles through which he could see the world as it really was.

Teddy's father, who was a wealthy merchant, realized that the double handicap his son had to bear — extreme near-sightedness and chronic asthma — could be helped by vigorous play and exercise. He had a gymnasium fixed up in the house* and Teddy worked hours on the punching bag, dumbbells, and horizontal bars.

He learned how to box and gain confidence in himself. He was by no means a natural athlete, but by steady work he gradually built up his body to the point where he could compete with other boys in athletics. Once in a boxing tournament held by his teacher, an ex-prizefighter, Teddy won a pewter cup in the lightweight class. It was persistence and courage rather than skill that enabled him to win the cup. These were forever the outstanding traits of his character — courage and persistence.

At fifteen his asthma had greatly improved, although he was still on the skinny side. But he knew then that the strenuous outdoor life was to be his. It led to strength and endurance and these were what he sought more than anything else. He grew up to admire men of action — athletes, hunters, fighting men. He became one of them himself, or rather all of them.

At the same time he did not neglect his mind. He was a man of great intellectual power, the author of more than thirty books during his lifetime. The wide range of subjects in his books reveals his many-sided character. Among the titles are: *The Naval War of 1812, The Deer Family, Through the Brazilian Wilderness, The Life of Oliver Cromwell, The Winning of the West, History as Literature,* and *African Game Trails.*

Just before his eighteenth birthday he entered Harvard. A frail-looking youth with pipestem legs, he weighed under 130 pounds and stood about five feet, eight. He became a whirlwind of activity at Harvard, with an endless enthusiasm for almost everything that went on.

He was a member of several societies and clubs, and he read papers before learned groups on poetry, politics, finance, and history. He was an editor of the *Harvard Advocate,* a member of the Rifle Club (he practiced target shooting by the hour), and he taught Sunday school. He drove a buggy, rowed on the Charles, ran, went on hikes, acted in a play, hunted in Maine, wrestled and boxed. He started work on his first book — the one on the War of 1812 — and

* The Roosevelt home at 28 East 20th Street, New York City, is now a museum. Everything in it, including the gymnasium, remains as it was 100 years ago.

he began the movement that led to track meets between Yale and Harvard. He was elected to Phi Beta Kappa.

He was too light for sports like football, crew, and baseball, but he went out for boxing and battled his way to the final in the college championship tournament, lightweight class. In this bout he was defeated by a taller and stronger man named Hanks. Roosevelt was handicapped by his eyesight as well as his weight. "You should have seen that little fellow staggering about banging the air," one of his classmates recalled with admiration. "Hanks couldn't put him out and Roosevelt wouldn't give up. It wasn't a fight, but, oh, he showed himself a fighter." He was always game.

Just before he graduated he went to a physician for a final physical examination. He was told that he had heart trouble and that he must choose a profession that would not demand much exertion. He was not supposed to exercise at all, not even to run upstairs.

A few months later, on his honeymoon in the Alps, Teddy climbed the dangerous Matterhorn to equal the feat of two boastful Englishmen who had recently scaled the mountain. He had apparently forgotten what the doctor had told him.

Following a brief career in New York politics, he decided to go out west and become a cowpuncher. He invested $50,000 in a ranch in the Dakota Territory Badlands, a region as rough and tough as its name.

He was a tenderfoot, an eastern dude, and the cowpunchers let him know it. For the first time since his boyhood he heard himself called "Four-eyes."

"Among strangers," he wrote in his autobiography, "I always had to spend twenty-four hours a day in living down the fact that I wore spectacles, remaining as long as I could judiciously deaf to any side remarks about 'four-eyes,' unless it became evident that my being quiet was misconstrued and that it was better to bring matters to a head at once."

By bringing matters to a head, which meant putting up his fists and offering to fight, he won the respect and admiration of the cowboys, some of whom were gunfighters.

He learned to ride as well as any plainsman and how to care for his horses. Often he would be in the saddle for days at a time, riding alone across the vast prairies in search of lost cattle.

Teddy Roosevelt in cowboy attire. This photograph was taken when he was a young ranch owner in the wild Dakota Territory.

He became a fine rifle shot. On various hunting expeditions to provision his ranch, he shot moose, grizzly bears, deer, elk, antelope, and buffalo. He also hunted wolves and mountain lions.

Roosevelt saw the closing day of the real wild west. He was there just before the last Indian wars were fought, when highwaymen still held up stagecoaches and horse thieves were hanged on the spot.

Teddy had a couple of close shaves. Once while riding alone he was seen by a small band of Indians from the top of a ridge. Suddenly they whipped out their guns and raced toward him at full speed. Teddy dismounted quickly and stood with his rifle ready. When they were about a hundred yards off he drew a bead on the first Indian.

"In a twinkling every man was lying over the side of his horse, and all had turned and were galloping backwards," he recalled later. "Indians — and for that matter, white men — do not like to ride in on a man who is cool and means shooting."

Roosevelt's coolness probably saved his life another time. He was on his way to the dining room in a small hotel when he heard two shots fired in the barroom. Teddy walked in and saw a man with a cocked gun in each hand. He had evidently been shooting at the clock which had two holes in its face.

The moment he spotted Teddy he announced to the crowd, "Four-eyes is going to treat." Teddy laughed and tried to get out of his way, but the gunman swore at him and again loudly ordered "Four-eyes" to buy drinks for the house.

Teddy grinned and said, "Well, if I've got to, I've got to," and looked past his tormentor toward the bar as if he were going there. At that instant he unleashed a terrific right-hand punch that landed on the man's jaw, then quickly followed it with his left and right.

Colonel Roosevelt leads the Rough Riders in a victorious charge up San Juan Hill during the Spanish-American War in 1898.

The gunman toppled over, firing both guns as he did, but the shots went wild. On the way down his head crashed against the corner of the bar and he went out cold. Teddy took away his guns. Later, when the man came to, he went directly to the station and left town on the next freight train.

The Dakotans thought so much of the vigorous young easterner that they made him a sheriff. Teddy was then in his late twenties and he had long since reached his full height of five feet, ten inches. He had filled out to a solid 140 pounds and he was in top physical condition.

It was a great life out there in the west, but it could not last. The ranch was a big money-loser and after four years Teddy sold it at a loss. Just before he left he wrote a friend in the east: "And so, let this letter serve as something of a notice. Tomorrow I am leaving for the east to return to public life. Hopefully, Sheriff Teddy."

The sheriff was made police commissioner of New York City, and after a few years he was called to Washington to become the Assistant Secretary of the Navy under President McKinley. He was serving in that office at the outbreak of the Spanish-American War.

A desk job was not for Teddy in time of war. He resigned from his high position and formed a volunteer cavalry regiment named the Rough Riders.* It was a colorful outfit, as tough and varied an aggregation of men as ever assembled in the United States. Among them were cowboys, professional gamblers, athletes from Yale and Harvard, mountaineers, stage drivers, clergymen, and broncobusters.

It didn't matter to Teddy where the men came from or what they did as long as they were good shots and good riders. His Rough Riders captured the imagination of the country.

Lieutenant Colonel Roosevelt stole the spotlight from higher-ranking officers by leading his men up San Juan Hill in Cuba in the face of heavy fire. The Rough Riders put the Spaniards to rout and took the hill, thus placing the American army on high ground overlooking Santiago.

Roosevelt was breveted brigadier general "for gallantry in action" and when he returned to the United States in 1898 he found himself a popular hero.

---

* A rough rider is a person who breaks horses so that they can be ridden; a broncobuster.

Teddy hardly had time to settle down before he was handed the Republican nomination for the governorship of New York. He was elected by a large majority and served for two years. In 1900 he accepted the nomination for vice-president as the running mate of President McKinley in his campaign for a second term. They won easily and Roosevelt found himself back in Washington again.

Six months after the inauguration, Roosevelt was in the heart of the Adirondack Mountains on vacation when a guide brought him a telegram to the effect that McKinley was dying. He had been badly wounded by a crazed assassin in Buffalo, New York. Roosevelt hastened to the city but did not arrive there until thirteen hours after McKinley's death. He took the oath of office in Buffalo. He served out that term and in 1904 he was elected in his own right.

There was something doing every second when the Roosevelt family lived in the White House, from 1901 to 1909. Teddy, as the President was called the country over, took more exercise than a prizefighter in a training camp. He worked out daily in the gymnasium installed in the White House.

He punched the bag, skipped rope, and pulled the weights. He boxed with numerous sparring partners, but his favorite was Professor Mike Donovan, a former world middleweight champion. He gave up boxing, however, when a navy officer hit him a hard blow on the forehead that caused a hemorrhage and permanently blinded his left eye.

He spread a wrestling mat on the gym floor and took jujitsu and wrestling lessons. He played tennis and went on long hikes.

While he was doing all this, his six children had the run of the place. They gave big parties, collected menageries and aquariums, and walked on tall stilts all over the White House. Once they shoved their pet pony into the elevator and carried him up to the third floor where they let him out in the hall.

M. Jusserand, the newly appointed French ambassador, was aghast at the strenuous life Teddy led. He wrote the following account of it in a dispatch sent to Paris soon after his arrival in this country:

"President Roosevelt invited me to take a promenade with him this afternoon at three. I arrived at the White House punctually, in afternoon dress and silk hat, as if we were to stroll in the Tuileries

First he chops down a few trees.

Then takes a cross-country canter.

And a twenty-minute brisk walk.

After which he gives the children a wheel-barrow ride.

He then rests for a moment

By which time he is ready for breakfast.

A humorous view of President Roosevelt's strenuous life, as seen by cartoonist McCutcheon in the Chicago *Tribune*.

Garden or in the Champs Elysées. To my surprise, the President soon joined me in a tramping suit, with knickerbockers and thick boots, and soft felt hat, much worn. Two or three other gentlemen came and we started off at what seemed to me a breakneck pace, which soon brought us out of the city.

"On reaching the country, the President went pell-mell over the fields, following neither road nor path, always on, on, straight ahead! I was much winded, but I would not give in, nor ask him to slow up, because I had the honor of *la belle France* in my heart. At last we came to the bank of a stream, rather wide and too deep to be forded. I sighed relief, because I thought that now we had reached our goal and would rest a moment and catch our breath before turning homeward.

"But judge of my horror when I saw the President unbutton his clothes and heard him say, 'We had better strip, so as not to wet our things in the creek.' Then I, too, for the honor of France, removed my apparel, everything except my lavender kid gloves. The President cast an inquiring look at these as if they, too, must come off, but I quickly forestalled any remark by saying, 'With your permission, Mr. President, I will keep these on; otherwise it would be embarrassing if we should meet ladies.' And so, we jumped into the water and swam across."

When Roosevelt was in office, baseball came of age with the establishment of the American League and the playing of the first World Series. Football, however, was losing ground in popular favor. It came very close to going out of existence.

It was a game of shove-and-pull, of mass power plays which, by their very nature, produced slugging, injuries, and unsportsmanlike conduct on the field. So brutal was the game that in one season alone (1905) eighteen players were killed. Today there are at least twenty times more college football players than there were then, and there are far fewer injuries and fatalities.

Roosevelt was among the first to realize that the game was in danger of killing itself. In 1905 he summoned representatives of Harvard, Yale, and Princeton to the White House and demanded that the game be freed of its bone-crushing brutality and foul play. These universities, known as the Big Three, were the first to play the game and they had always made its rules. The President pounded the table with his fist in typical Roosevelt fashion and told the Big Three to change the rules.

The result was the formation of the American Football Rules Committee, and the introduction in 1906 of plays designed to open up the game and make it less dangerous to play.

The forward pass was introduced, the distance to be gained on downs was increased from five yards to ten, and all mass formations were prohibited. The new rules, thanks in great part to President Roosevelt, worked wonders. Not only did injuries and deaths decrease, but the game proved to be more interesting to watch and more fun to play.

When Teddy left the White House he sailed for Africa with his twenty-two-year-old son Kermit to hunt big game. They made one of the first hunting safaris in East Africa.

Today an African safari is well organized and is almost as comfortable as staying home. There are ice boxes, even freezers and portable showers. Iced drinks are always ready. Baggage and equipment are carried by trucks. Land-rovers range far and wide with the hunters. There is constant radio communication between the safari and Nairobi, the headquarters city.

A cartoon of Teddy as the mighty African hunter.

Roosevelt (shown here as an animal tamer) subdues the brutal football slugger and cleans up the game. Some of his other victims appear in the background.

The Roosevelt safari was nothing like that. There were no roads and no bridges across the rivers. The Roosevelts walked and rode horseback. They swam across the rivers. The baggage and equipment were carried on the heads of the native porters, who walked bare-footed all the way. There was no ice, there were no portable showers, and there was no communication with the outside world.

Teddy, the redoubtable hunter and skilled outdoorsman, enjoyed every minute of the safari. He carried with him a rabbit's foot which his friend, John L. Sullivan, had given him for luck. The charm worked.

The Roosevelts killed more than 500 animals and birds, including seventeen lions and several rhinos, elephants, hippopotami, and giraffes. The Smithsonian Institution in Washington later mounted and exhibited fifty of their best trophies.

Out of the safari came Roosevelt's classic hunting book, *African Game Trails*. He wrote it partly to pay the costs of the hunt and partly to satisfy his desire to write about everything he did.

Teddy Roosevelt was our most unusual president in many ways. No other president had so many accomplishments, or fitted so many successful careers into one lifetime. He played many parts and played them well. The amazing many-sidedness of Roosevelt appealed to all manner of men.

His Secretary of State, John M. Hay, who years before had been Abraham Lincoln's private secretary, wrote of President Roosevelt: "Of gentle birth and breeding, yet a man of the people . . . with the training of a scholar and the breezy accessibility of a ranchman; a man of the library and a man of the world; an athlete and a thinker; a soldier and a statesman . . . with the sensibility of a poet and the steel nerve of a rough rider."

There was one more adventure in store for Teddy. Three years after his return from Africa he led an expedition into the jungles of Brazil, where he explored 900 miles of an unknown river. His party suffered great hardship and many were laid low with tropical

A sketch of Roosevelt drawn in 1914 by James Montgomery Flagg.

fever. Teddy himself became very ill. Unselfishly he urged the others to go on and leave him to die, as he did not want to be a burden on them. But they refused to do so.

For forty-eight hours he was very close to death, until his fever at last broke. With great effort he got on his feet and started out with his companions. They had to cut their way through the jungle. There were no trails and their dugout canoes had long since been smashed in the rapids. Sometimes Roosevelt could barely crawl.

They went along this way for several days, until they came to a level plain where there were no more rapids. There, they rested and got their strength back. The Brazilian porters built new dugouts and once more they started on down the river toward civilization.

The mysterious jungle river that swallowed the explorers for so many weeks has since been named the Río Teodoro by the Brazilian government.

The two men who succeeded Roosevelt to the presidency belong to his era. They were William Howard Taft and Woodrow Wilson in that order and they deserve mention as presidents who liked sports.

The three presidents were totally unlike one another in build and in temperament but they did have some things in common. All three were sports enthusiasts; they were graduates of the Big Three (Taft went to Yale, Wilson to Princeton), and they ran against each other for president in the bitter three-party campaign of 1912.

Big Bill Taft, a kindly giant of enormous proportions, was our largest president. He stood almost six feet and weighed about 350 pounds at his fleshy peak.

As a youngster in Cincinnati he played some sand-lot baseball, but by the time he reached Yale in the fall of 1874 he was too fat for athletics. There were not many college sports to choose from, anyway, in those days. Football was just beginning at Yale and there was little interest in it. The only organized sports were crew and baseball.

When Taft graduated in 1878, the average weight of his class-mates was 151 pounds. He was weighed on graduation day and scaled 225 pounds. He kept climbing from there.

Despite his size, Taft made history of a sort as a presidential pioneer in sports. A devoted baseball fan, he was the first president to throw out a ball to open the major-league season. This he did in Washington on April 14, 1910,* thus establishing a custom that has been continued by every president since then.

Big Bill was the first president to play golf seriously.** Although his game was atrocious, it afforded him good exercise and he kept hacking away at the ball for many years.

He also rode horseback for exercise. When he was governor of the Philippines in 1903, disturbing reports about his poor health got back to Washington. This caused Secretary of War Elihu Root to send him an inquiry by cable.

The blimp-like Taft cabled back that his health was excellent. He had just finished a twenty-five-mile horseback ride and was feeling fine. Secretary Root smiled and cabled back: "How is the horse?"

Woodrow Wilson was a professor of political economy in three colleges and the president of Princeton University before he entered politics. He was cold, aloof, and intellectual rather than muscular. Yet he had a lifelong interest in sports and a boyish admiration for the athletic heroes of the college campus and the professional baseball field.

"There was something in the struggle of stern men that set his blood going," wrote his biographer, R. S. Baker.

He was handicapped by a frail physique and poor eyesight, but despite this, Wilson was a baseball player, golfer, and football coach. He performed only briefly in these activities (with the exception of golf) and he did not shine at any.

His baseball-playing career, for example, lasted but one season — the spring of 1874 when he was a seventeen-year-old freshman at

* The game was between Washington and Philadelphia. It was seen by a crowd of 12,226, which was an attendance record for Washington at that time.

** President William McKinley played a few holes of golf in White Sulphur Springs, West Virginia, when he was on vacation there in 1899, but he did not continue with the game.
Teddy Roosevelt never played golf and could not understand why any man would want to play it. He said it was a woman's game.

President Taft throws out the first ball to open the 1910 baseball season. He established this custom which has been continued by every President who followed him.

Davidson College in North Carolina. Tommy, as he was then called (he was christened Thomas Woodrow Wilson), played center field on the college nine. He was an average batter but he lacked the competitive spirit. "Tommy Wilson would be a good player if he wasn't so lazy!" said his team captain, Robert Glenn, of the scholarly, languid youth. Delicate health rather than laziness may have been the cause of his indifferent play on the field.

He suffered a near physical breakdown at the end of the school term and stayed home convalescing for more than a year. But he never lost interest in the game. He transferred to Princeton and in his senior year there (1879) he was chosen president of the baseball association. Later, as a professor, he delighted in watching "the splendid games between the crack professional nines of the country."

Football captured the interest of the bespectacled and dignified professor of history at Wesleyan University in Connecticut. He plunged with enthusiasm into college athletics and took a hand at

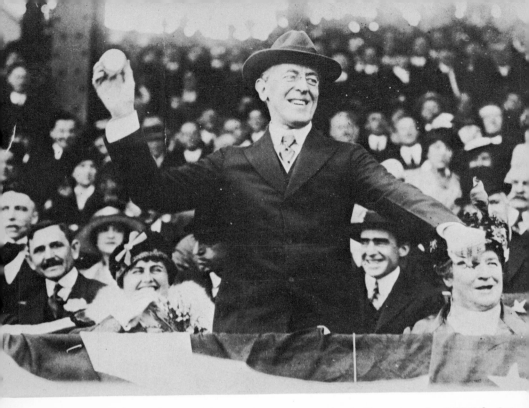

President Woodrow Wilson tossed out the ball to start the 1915 Series between the Red Sox and the Phillies. He was the first President to attend a World Series game.

coaching the team. It is doubtful if he taught the players very much, but he was certainly the team's chief rooter.

"Go in to win; don't admit defeat before you start," he used to yell. One time, the story goes, he ran out onto the field bellowing about the injustice of a decision against Wesleyan in a football game with Amherst.

In 1890, in Wilson's first year as a professor of history at Princeton, he took a turn at coaching the football team. Edgar Poe, one of the famous Poe brothers who played for Princeton, was the captain that year. He later said that Professor Wilson's coaching was "inspiring but not instructive." After a season that ended with a 32-to-0 loss to Yale, Wilson gave up football coaching for good.

He took up golf and continued to play throughout his life. Like Taft, he played a terrible but good-humored game and was generally well over 100. Golf to him was a form of exercise rather than a contest and he was undisturbed by his sky-high scores.

Attired in sweater and cap, Wilson would leave the White House in the morning promptly at 8:30, arrive at the golf course ten minutes later, and spend a couple of hours whacking the ball around. He would then drive back to the White House, take a shower, and dress for his eleven o'clock appearance at his office.

Wilson once said of his game: "My right eye is like a horse's. I can see straight out with it but not sideways. As a result, I cannot take a full swing because my nose gets in the way and cuts off my view of the ball. That's why I use such a short swing."

The day after the 1916 election, which Wilson won, he was on the golf course with Admiral Clay Grayson when they encountered some players near the eighteenth hole.

"How is your game today, Mr. President?" one of them called out. Wilson waved his hand and smiled, "The Admiral has me three down, but I don't care. I am four states up on yesterday's election."

Wilson may not have burned with a champion's zeal, but he had fun playing golf, and fun as a sports fan.

The three presidents of this era were all born within a span of two years (1856–1858) and they were in college at the same time. According to life expectancy tables and also medical opinion, the one who exercised the most and kept in the best physical shape through clean, outdoor living would be the choice to outlive the others; the one who let himself go physically to become grossly overweight would be expected to die first.

Strangely, however, just the opposite was true in the case of these presidents. Roosevelt, the youngest of the trio and the most physically fit, died first at the age of sixty. Wilson, who had no bad habits and whose weight was just right for his height, was the next to go, at sixty-seven. The fattest, unhealthiest, and most out-of-shape was Taft, who lived to be seventy-two and died in 1930. He outlived Roosevelt by eleven years and Wilson by six.

President Harding, golfer and baseball fan, greets the great Yankee slugger, Babe Ruth.

Sports for Everyone

WARREN G. HARDING, a large, genial man who succeeded Woodrow Wilson, was the third consecutive golfing president. It was his delight to practice approach shots on the south grounds of the White House with his pet Scottie, Laddie Boy, beside him. Every time he made a shot the dog would bolt for the ball, seize it in his mouth, and bring it back to the President.

On the golf course Harding always wore plus fours (loose knickerbockers), the standard golfing costume of that time. He generally played at the Chevy Chase Club near Washington or on the private course of Friendship, the home of the Hardings' wealthy friends, the Edward B. McLeans.

There is no doubt that the three golfing presidents helped popularize the game. When Taft first took up golf, it was generally considered to be a game for wealthy people of middle age and above. It was confined to a few exclusive country clubs, most of which were in the eastern part of the United States. The world's best players came from the British Isles. They won almost all the tournaments held in this country, and there was scarcely a club professional in America who was not a Briton or a Scot.

Although the presidents stimulated some interest in the game, its rise to nation-wide popularity could not be attributed entirely to

Golf and tennis did not gain popularity until after the first World War. Many saw golf as an old man's game, or one for a dude, as this cartoon of the golf "idiot" indicates.

Tennis was a study in slow motion until the cannon ball serve was introduced in 1912 (opposite page).

them. An event that took place in 1913 when Wilson was president gave the game its greatest lift and put it on the American sports pages forever.

This was the United States Open Championship, played at the Country Club in Brookline, Massachusetts, where an unknown twenty-year-old ex-caddy named Francis Ouimet tied the heavily favored British professionals, Harry Vardon and Ted Ray, in the final round and then beat both of them in the playoff with a stunning 72.

Ouimet, a poor boy and an amateur who lived across the street from the Country Club, had achieved the impossible. He had vanquished the world's two greatest professionals, one of whom (Vardon) had won the British Open five times.

In the playoff the whole country was rooting for young Ouimet. As soon as he won, thousands of people across the nation realized for the first time that golf was not just a rich old man's pastime. It was a fine competitive game, one that anyone could play regardless of age or social background.

Ouimet's famous victory has been called the "Shots Heard 'Round the World" because of the tremendous impetus it gave to the game. When he won the championship in 1913 there were some 35,000

golfers in the United States. More than two million people were playing the game less than ten years later when Harding became president. Today there are about four million American golfers.

Tennis also rose to new heights of popularity following World War I, thanks in great part to a new and exciting star who, like Ouimet, was considered an "outsider." He was Maurice M. McLoughlin, the "California Comet," who burst upon the scene with a new style of play and changed the game almost overnight.

Before the redheaded McLoughlin came east in 1912 to win the National Championship, tennis was a rather slow and cautious game. The power serve was unknown and only a few players ventured to the net. Many people considered it a sissy game, played mostly by eastern college youths. (Teddy Roosevelt tried tennis a few times but found it too slow and gave it up.)

McLoughlin's game was a revelation. He thrilled eastern crowds with his dashing style of play — his cannonball serves and rushes to the net, his volleying and speed of foot. He added power and color to the game and became a great favorite with the crowds. They came to see him play in ever-increasing numbers. McLoughlin awakened the country to tennis. No longer was it sneered at as a pitty-pat, girlish game.

President Harding died suddenly of a stroke in the summer of 1923, in the middle of his only term of office. He was succeeded by Vice-President Calvin Coolidge, who remained in the White House until 1929.

Thus, the terms of these two presidents spanned the 1920's, which were the most remarkable decade in the history of American sports. Never before or since has there been such a concentration of athletic genius in so many different sports. It was a time of superb performances, public idolatry of sports heroes, and fabulous purses.

Among the great champions who reigned during this period, which is known as America's Golden Age of Sports, were: Babe Ruth, baseball's greatest slugger; Jack Dempsey, the most destructive heavyweight the ring has known; Red Grange, football's finest running back and three years an All-American. Golf produced the peerless Bobby Jones, whose feats have never been equaled. Big Bill Tilden and Helen Wills were virtually unbeatable on the tennis courts for ten years, and at swimming no one could touch Johnny Weismuller at any distance between fifty yards and a half mile. In track, sprinter Charlie Paddock stood by himself as the "World's Fastest Human." Polo produced the greatest player of all time in Tommy Hitchcock. And so it went in almost every sport.

All these superstars and many others came at the same time. Accounts of their magnificent performances crowded the front pages of the newspapers. For example, when Gene Tunney defeated Jack Dempsey for the heavyweight crown on September 23, 1926, the New York *Times* next day devoted its entire front page to the story of the fight.

It is doubtful if President Coolidge, an unsmiling Vermonter, was much aware of what was going on in sports, for he was not interested in them. He was, perhaps, the most complete non-sportsman ever to enter the White House.

It was a different story, though, when he moved out of the White House five and a half years later. He was a sportsman when he left — maybe not a full-fledged one, but at least he took up sports for the first time when he became president and learned to enjoy them. In this he was most unusual, and unlike any other president.

The man who awakened Coolidge to sports was Colonel Edmund W. Starling, the commander of the Secret Service men charged with

92

guarding the presidents. Colonel Starling had first served under President Wilson and he had been closely associated with him and with Harding.

It was part of his job to know the presidents' tastes and habits, as well as their favorite sports and hobbies. He often acted as a companion to them and sometimes filled in as a golf partner. Starling was well equipped for the job. He was an all-round sportsman — a fly fisherman, a crack shot, a golfer, and an accomplished horseman. He served five presidents in all, ending with Franklin D. Roosevelt.

When he retired he wrote a book entitled *Starling of the White House*, in which he gave much space to Calvin Coolidge, his favorite president. He admitted, however, that he had some trying moments in his first talks with Coolidge when he tried to find out about the new president's daily routine, his hobbies and sports.

"I was distressed to find out that he took no other exercise except walking," wrote Starling. "He did not play golf, ride horseback, fish, hunt, swim, bowl or even play billiards. He had no hobbies, not even stamp collecting. Moreover, he walked with his head thrust forward, his hands clasped behind him."

This was no way to take exercise, Starling gently explained to the President. He told Coolidge that to get the full benefit of walking he should stride with his head up, chest out, take deep breaths and move his arms. "Silent Cal," as the President was known because he did not talk much, listened in silence to Starling's advice.

The next time the two men went out together for a stroll, Starling was astonished at the President's new walking style. He was also amused. Silent Cal started off briskly like a competitor in a walking race. He thrust out his chest, squared his shoulders, held his head high and breathed deeply. He waved his arms wildly about with every step. Starling drew back, then fell behind to avoid getting sideswiped by the President's thrashing arms.

Thus started Coolidge's education in outdoor activities under the tutelage of Colonel Starling. Lessons in other fields were to follow. Silent Cal would prove to be an apt pupil.

"Silent Cal" may have been the nation's nickname for Coolidge, but around the White House behind his back he was known as the "Little Fellow." The name was not spoken in scorn by his aides. It

Unsmiling Cal Coolidge, attired in business suit and rubber boots, does not appear to enjoy his role as trout fisherman.

was more of an affectionate term. Cal was well liked by those who were close to him.

Actually, the reddish-haired, brown-eyed President was not little. He was of medium height, standing about five feet, nine inches, but he was thin and slight in build. He *seemed* to be little, especially in comparison with the much larger and taller Harding whom he followed into the White House.

Silent Cal took a big stride forward in the sports world one summer when he went on vacation at Lake Osgood in the Adirondacks and learned how to fish. It is doubtful if he had ever fished before, even as a farm boy in the back hills of Vermont.

Colonel Starling was his constant companion at Lake Osgood and he persuaded the President to try his hand at fishing. He had to be taught everything — how to handle the rod and reel, how to bait his hook and cast, and what to do when he got a bite.

Coolidge was a reluctant pupil at first and rather suspicious of the whole idea. But from the moment he caught his first fish — it turned out to be a five-pound pike — he wanted to do nothing else but fish. He insisted on fishing every day with Starling. "He became the most ardent fisherman I have ever known," Starling wrote.

In 1927 the Coolidges spent the summer at the South Dakota State Game Lodge in the Black Hills. This, incidentally, was the first time a president had ever gone west of the Mississippi River for his summer vacation.

Rhodes Creek ran by the lodge and it was supposedly good trout water. But Starling wanted to make sure that Cal got good fishing. One night he secretly dumped a lot of rainbow trout into the creek. He made sure they wouldn't get away by sinking steel mesh nets across the stream above and below the lodge. He had logs placed on top of the nets to conceal them. The President would never know that the creek had been stocked.

A few days later the two men went fishing. Before they started off, several reporters and photographers clustered around them taking pictures and asking questions. Coolidge readily admitted to the reporters that he was not a fly fisherman and that he intended to use worms and grasshoppers.

There was a great outcry over this by the nation's fly fishermen, many thousands of whom consider it unsportsmanlike to use anything but flies for trout. Silent Cal was not disturbed by this. He wanted to catch fish and the best way to do it, in his opinion, was the way the Vermonters did it — with worms.

However, when he saw Starling get some big trout with a fly while he went empty-handed with worms and grasshoppers, he decided to try fly fishing. Starling taught him how to cast a fly, but the President never became very good at it.

It is said that he gave his Secret Service guards some lively moments dodging his back cast and removing flies from trees, bushes, and even from his own clothes. Cal was more at home with worms.

During his Black Hills vacation, Coolidge was given a horse and he insisted on riding it, although he had not been astride one since his boyhood days on the farm. Starling knew that the animal was nervous and frisky and he was afraid that it might throw the President and seriously injure him. He explained this to Silent Cal, who, as usual, listened without saying anything.

"I could see what he was thinking," Starling later wrote. "Just because he was President he believed he could get on a horse and miraculously be able to ride. (They all do. They think the title of President is a magic wand which changes them into great horsemen, great fishermen, great hunters, etc.)."

In the end Starling persuaded Coolidge to give up the nervous horse and, if he must ride, try a steadier one. The name of the gentle horse was Mistletoe. The President went to the stables and looked the horse over, patted him and fed him candy. He announced that he would ride Mistletoe that very afternoon.

Attired in cowboy's clothes, including a ten-gallon western hat, Coolidge mounted Mistletoe and rode off with Starling and some other Secret Service men. His companions set a slow pace and under their watchful eye no harm came to the President. Thereafter he rode daily. Before the summer was over he became a passable horseman.

When he returned to the White House he found a substitute for Mistletoe. It was an electric horse, a gift from one of his admirers. Cal had it installed in his bedroom and summoned Starling to see it.

The President then mounted the horse, pressed a button, and held on. The horse rocked and bucked and almost sent Cal flying. He was delighted with it, however, and from then on he rode it every afternoon. Starling always attended these indoor riding sessions. The two men would take turns mounting the mechanical horse and they would laugh at each other like a couple of schoolboys. Starling said it was great fun and good exercise.

The Secret Service Chief did not think that the President's sports education would be complete until he had learned to shoot, but he knew that he could not talk Mr. Coolidge into taking lessons. The President would have to be shown. Carefully, Starling laid his plans.

One day he casually suggested to the President that he might like to watch some Secret Service men shoot clay pigeons on a range near the Black Hills lodge. Coolidge nodded his head affirmatively. A few days later, after arrangements had been made, he was brought to the scene of the shoot.

The men staged a good show for him. Rarely did they miss a bird as it flew from the trap. Starling watched the President out of the corner of his eye and knew that he was being impressed. For over an hour Silent Cal watched the men shoot but he did not utter a single word. Finally, when it was time to leave, he spoke for the first time. "I want to shoot," he said to Starling and left for the lodge.

The next day Starling gave the President his first shooting lesson. The President readily took to the new sport. He shot every day and was a willing pupil. Although he never became a really good shot, he did well enough to be classed as "average." And that was not bad for a man who had never handled a gun until he had passed his fifty-fifth birthday.

Later, when Coolidge went hunting in the field, he was able to get his share of live birds. Starling accompanied him one time on a shooting trip to Sapelo Island, Georgia, for quail and pheasant.

The President shot well, Starling recalled with understandable pride. He was better at bringing down pheasant than quail, which fly much faster than pheasant and are smaller.

The important thing was that Coolidge enjoyed the sport, just as he enjoyed fishing and riding. Calvin Coolidge bloomed late in life as a lover of sports but he got great satisfaction from them. He left the White House a healthier and happier man because of his interest in sports.

This portrait of Herbert Clark Hoover was painted in 1921, seven years before he was elected president.

Herbert C. Hoover, the next president, was a ready-made sports-man before he ever saw the White House. A solidly built man with a square face, he was an expert fly fisherman who would not think of using worms for trout. He also was a baseball and football fan and he was well informed on these games.

Hoover was the first president born west of the Mississippi River. The son of a Quaker blacksmith, he entered the world in a small frame house in West Branch, Iowa, on August 10, 1874.

His early boyhood was a mixture of joy and sadness. When he was a candidate for the presidency he made a speech in which he mentioned some of the gayest memories of his boyhood. He recalled the swimming hole under the willows in West Branch and the ball games he played "with a shaped hickory stick for a bat and a ball made by winding yarn around a piece of rubber." He remembered skating on the swimming hole in winter and fishing there in summer with a willow pole, a line made of butcher's string and a penny hook baited with a piece of angleworm "spit on . . . to make the fish bite."

He also remembered — but he did not mention this in his speech — the grief he knew when both his parents died. He was an orphan at the age of nine.

The youngster was brought up by relatives in Oregon. At seven-teen he entered Stanford University in California and worked his way through for four years.

In the fall of 1892, when Hoover was a sophomore, the University of California challenged Stanford to a football game. California had played high school and club teams but had never played another college. Stanford did not even have a regular team. Nevertheless, Stanford accepted the challenge and the students began to put a team together.

They chose young Hoover to make the arrangements for the game. There was a lot of work to be done, but Hoover, a good organizer, did the job well. He ordered new uniforms — on credit against the gate receipts. He had 5,000 tickets printed (priced at $2 each) and rented a baseball park in San Francisco for $250.

Surprisingly, the game was a sellout. It was the Far West's first intercollegiate football game and interest ran high. More than 5,000 people jammed the stands to see the beginning of the Stanford-

California football rivalry. The game now attracts crowds up to 80,000 fans every fall.

The players took the field and the boisterous throng sounded off with yells, horns, and rattles. At last everything was ready for the kickoff. But instead of lining up, the players stood around without doing anything. Soon, amid a mighty silence, they began walking off the field. It then dawned on the crowd what had happened. There was no football!

Horrified, Hoover begged a sporting goods dealer to drive to his store in town and get a football. It was an hour before the unhappy man returned to the field with a makeshift football. He had a pigskin in his store but he did not have a bladder for it. Hurriedly he put a punching bag bladder in it and somehow inflated it to make a lopsided football.

The game finally started. Although there were some fumbles because of the misshapen football, it was a good game and the crowd liked it. Stanford won, 14-10.

Hoover and his assistants spent most of the night counting receipts in his hotel room. They stuffed nearly $20,000 into cloth bags and put them under the mattress of Hoover's bed. Not until then was the future president able to relax and remember that he had been too busy to see the game.

Hoover became an efficient engineer with a genius for organization. His career took him all over the world. By the time he was forty he had a chain of offices encircling the globe and had amassed a fortune.

He was elected president on the eve of the Great Depression, which became world-wide and as unstoppable as a hurricane, but be was blamed for it just the same. As the depression deepened, his popularity diminished. Once he suffered the indignity of being publicly booed at a baseball game.

His only relaxation during his single term of office (1929–1933) was in fishing. He turned over the presidential yacht, *Mayflower*, to the Navy and he did away with the White House stables as measures of economy. He accepted no salary while he was president.

He gave up every recreation but fishing. It was his delight to motor to his camp on the Rapidan River in the Virginia mountains about 100 miles from the White House and spend the weekend there. He would wade the river and fish it in the classic manner, with a light trout rod and flies. He preferred to be alone.

"Presidents have only two moments of personal seclusion. One is prayer; the other is fishing — and they cannot pray all the time," he wrote in his book, *Fishing for Fun*.

To Hoover the sport meant a good deal more than merely catching fish. It meant communing with nature, breathing pure air, and seeing the shimmer of the sun on the blue waters. "It brings meekness," he once said in a speech, "and inspiration from the glory and wonder of nature. . . . And it brings rejoicing that you do not have to decide a darned thing until next week."

He was fond of quoting the following words which were written on an Assyrian tablet about four thousand years ago: *The Gods Do Not Subtract From the Allotted Span of Men's Lives the Hours Spent in Fishing.*

Hoover was perhaps the most skillful fisherman of all the presidents. His enthusiasm for the sport never waned. He fished until he was in his late eighties and he never seemed to lose his touch.

He was a member of the Anglers' Club in the Florida Keys and he went there for the bonefishing every winter for a number of years. It takes more skill to catch a bonefish than almost any other kind of fish.

In this country these fish are found only in south Florida. They live on the grassy flats in shallow water and they are extremely scary. The water is clear in the Keys and a fisherman in a boat can see the bonefish as they swim by looking for food. The bonefish can also see him. If he makes a sudden move and startles them they are off like lightning and are seen no more.

The angler, therefore, must cast with almost no motion the moment he sees the fish and he must place his bait, or fly, very gently in just the right place. If this is done well and the bonefish takes the lure, he puts up a terrific battle.

He is among the great gamefish of the world and sportsmen come from all over the country to seek him in the Keys. His average weight is about six pounds, but any bonefisherman will swear that the fighting fish feels more like a sixty-pounder when he is on the end of a line.

Hoover's guide for many years was Captain Calvin Albury of

Key Largo. The Captain has guided innumerable fishermen in his time and he says that Hoover is about the best one he ever took out. One time he fished with the ex-president for nineteen days in a row, from morning until late afternoon. In that time they caught 109 bonefish, but Hoover, like most bonefishermen, did not keep a single one. He released them all unharmed. (The bonefish is not good to eat and the only reason for keeping one would be to have it mounted and hung on the wall.)

At the end of the 1962 winter season, when Hoover was eighty-seven, he gave Captain Albury his wrist watch and his favorite rod and reel. The old gentleman said that he did not think he would be back again.

Following Hoover's defeat in the 1932 election, Franklin Delano Roosevelt moved into the White House. He stayed there more than twelve years, longer than any other president, until death struck him down in 1945.

FDR, as our thirty-second president was generally known, was Teddy Roosevelt's fifth cousin, and the two men had much in common. Each was born to considerable wealth, each went to Harvard, each served as assistant secretary of the Navy and governor of New York, and each was nominated vice-president of the United States before achieving the presidency.

As sports lovers, however, they had little in common. FDR was mildly interested in sports but that was about all. He led a sheltered life as a boy. He had a nurse and governesses who taught him to speak French and German. He had private tutors until he was fourteen, when he was sent to the exclusive Groton School in Massachusetts.

At Groton he went out for football but did not make the team. At Harvard his efforts in athletics were halfhearted. When he tried for the freshman football team, he failed to make it. The only other sport he took up was rowing, but he was not good enough for the varsity crew.

He had the physical equipment for athletics, but the desire was lacking. He was well built and stood two inches over six feet. In college he weighed about 170 pounds. He played some golf and rode horseback, but the sport that stirred him most was sailing. He was a good skipper and an expert craftsman with boats.

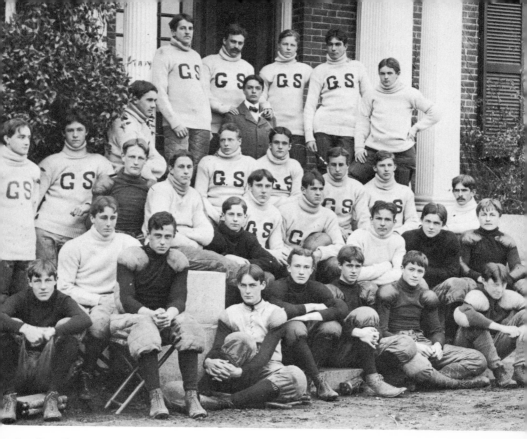

In this photograph of the 1899 Groton School football squad, Franklin D. Roosevelt is seated in the front row, second from the left, wearing a white sweater without letters.

The Roosevelt summer home was on Campobello Island, which is in New Brunswick, Canada, but only a mile or so off the coast of Maine. In those waters young Franklin learned to sail.

A cruise that he always remembered with pleasure was the one he took the summer before he entered Harvard, when he sailed out of Campobello in his own forty-foot yacht, the *Half Moon*. He was the skipper, in command of three other teenagers who made up the crew. They sailed along the coast of Maine, New Brunswick, and Nova Scotia.

Twenty-one years after that delightful summer cruise, Franklin Roosevelt, a lawyer aged thirty-nine and in vibrant health, was on vacation at Campobello with his wife and children when tragedy struck him. He suddenly fell ill and developed a high fever. The next morning he complained of acute pain in his legs. In two days they were paralyzed. A victim of infantile paralysis, Roosevelt never again stood on his feet unless he was supported by leg braces or crutches. Most of the time he was confined to a wheel chair.

The dreadful blow failed to crush his spirit. He was determined to continue his law practice and political career despite the terrible handicap.

The only way he could free himself of the burden of the sixty pounds of dead weight of his leg braces was through the buoyancy of water. A man is almost weightless in water.

Roosevelt went to Warm Springs, Georgia, where a pool is fed by an underground spring which has a constant temperature of eighty-eight degrees. In the pool he spent long hours taking leg exercises under the direction of a doctor. They seemed to help him and he returned again and again.

He was so enthusiastic about Warm Springs that he bought the entire property, including the hotel, cottage and pool, and 1,200 acres of land. The institution was incorporated as a nonprofit enterprise and it is in operation today.

Life never returned to his legs, but he relearned many things — how to drive an automobile, for example, and even to ride a horse once more. But there was so much that he could never do again. He could never go on a hike, skate, dance, or even climb a stair that was more than two or three inches high. If he dropped something he could not lean over and pick it up. He could not kneel to pray. There were thousands of other things a man with normal legs takes for granted that Roosevelt could not do for the rest of his life.

It has been said of Roosevelt that his paralysis was the beginning of a spiritual rebirth, that he was born again at the age of thirty-nine. At least it marked the beginning of a career that led to the presidency and to world-wide fame.

In the White House FDR derived much pleasure from the swimming pool that was built in 1933 and installed in the west terrace of the mansion. It is fifty feet long and fifteen feet wide and has a depth which varies from four and a half feet to eight feet. The walls are faced with terra-cotta of various shades of marine blue and green. The pool, which has a springboard at one end, has been used by every president since FDR.

Franklin D. Roosevelt and other patients in the enclosed pool at Warm Springs, Georgia, in 1928.

At Warm Springs, on April 12, 1945, a few months after FDR's fourth inauguration, he died suddenly from a stroke. That evening shortly after seven o'clock Vice-President Harry Truman was made President when he was sworn in by Chief Justice Harlan Fiske Stone.

Truman, the seventh accidental president, was never an athlete and did not engage in any sports except an occasional try at fishing. His only exercise consisted of brisk morning walks.

Truman's successor, however, was a good athlete in his youth and remains a lover of sports and games. He is Dwight D. Eisenhower, known fondly as Ike to millions of people.

Cadet "Ike" Eisenhower made the varsity football team at West Point in 1912, but an injury cut short his career.

Of all the presidents Ike was the most natural athlete, which means that he was born with athletic skills and ability. Sports came easily to him in contrast to Teddy Roosevelt, for example, who was not a natural athlete and had to endure agonizing hours of practice to achieve what he did in sports.

As a schoolboy in Abilene, Kansas, the slim, yellow-haired youngster with a ready smile was a leader in athletics. He was the best baseball and football player in Abilene High. He was also very handy with his fists, but he was never a bully.

Ike was the third of seven sons. His father was a mechanic in a creamery and his wages were small. The Eisenhowers lived in a nondescript frame house on the south side of town, in the poor section across the railroad tracks.

Schooldays were not all golden for the Eisenhower boys. They wore shabby, handed-down clothes, passed on from one brother to another, and their schoolmates often made fun of them. Ike suffered humiliation when he was forced to wear the high button-top shoes his mother had worn until they were almost beyond repair.

The boys from the north side of town ridiculed the Eisenhowers more than the south-siders did. The north-siders came from the wealthier families of Abilene and they lived in fine homes. Sometimes when Ike and his brothers were goaded beyond endurance, up would come the Eisenhower fists and there would be a brisk battle in the schoolyard. These flurries almost always ended in a quick Eisenhower victory.

"It made us scrappers," said one of Ike's brothers years later. "It was always us against odds. We developed a sort of feudal feeling."

It became a school tradition that there would be at least one major fight every year between a south side and a north side boy. Ike's older brothers, Arthur and Edgar, had each in turn been champions of the south side and they had won their battles against the champion north-siders. Ike's turn came next, when he was thirteen years old.

He was challenged by Wesley Merrifield, who was a thick-set boy and the acknowledged champion of the north side. He had the advantage over Ike in weight, reach, and strength. Few thought that Ike would have much chance against him.

There were no hard feelings between the two boys. It was not a grudge fight. It was the school's annual test match — similar, in a way, to the final of a boxing tournament, such as the one in which Teddy Roosevelt fought at Harvard.

There were definite rules for these fights at Garfield School in Abilene, although they were never written down. The boys were expected to fight "clean" and use their fists only. They must not wrestle or kick.

The fight took place after school on an October afternoon in a vacant lot across the street from the city hall. A large crowd of schoolchildren and men surrounded the fighters and formed a ring.

A few old-timers in Abilene who saw that battle still speak of it with awe today, more than sixty years later. It was, they say, the "toughest kid fight" the town ever saw.

It started off the way everyone expected it to go. Wes was the stronger. He landed solid punches on Ike's face and body and gave a lot more than he took. But Ike kept boring in without flinching. He was absolutely game.

They fought on. Twenty minutes passed, which was far beyond the time most fights lasted. But it was only the beginning of this amazing struggle. A half hour went by. Forty-five minutes. A full hour. Still they fought, but now they could hardly lift their aching arms. Both were badly battered, their eyes half closed, their lips puffed and bleeding.

The sun went down and they fought in semi-darkness. Both were so groggy that they could not do much but shove each other feebly with their fists. But neither would quit. At last, when the fight was more than two hours old, they came together for the final time and realized that it was useless to go on.

"Ike," gasped Wes, "I can't lick you." Ike managed to grin. "Well, Wes," he said, "I haven't licked you."

Ike staggered home and just managed to get upstairs to his room, where he collapsed on his bed. When Edgar entered the room and saw his younger brother's battered face he was beside himself with rage. "Who did it?" he stormed. "Tell me who did it."

Ike calmed him down. He told Edgar it had been a fair fight. It was Wes Merrifield. He was a great fighter and he fought clean, said Ike, and he had no complaints. For the next three days Ike stayed home. Only then was he able to go back to school.

108

In proper trout angler's attire, President Eisenhower, a keen fisherman, casts a fly in a mountain stream. (Compare Ike's costume with Cal Coolidge's on page 94.)

Ike had a high sense of justice and always insisted on fairness and clean play in sports. When he became Abilene High's star tackle and the mainstay of the football team, he would often take the lead in reprimanding any boy who had played "dirty." He was a rough player himself and he fought hard, but he was always "clean."

Ike also starred in baseball. He played right field and was the team's heaviest hitter.

After graduating from high school, Ike worked in the creamery for a year and then decided that he wanted a college education — a free one, if possible, for he could not afford to pay for one.

Through the Kansas senators he arranged to take the War Department competitive examinations for West Point or Annapolis. In those days a candidate taking the examinations could list himself as "either," meaning that he had no preference between the two service academies. He would accept an appointment to either one and leave it to the government to make the choice for him. In this way his chances of getting into one of them would be improved.

Ike passed the examinations with high marks and was appointed to West Point. He had hoped for a naval appointment. Later he found out that his age had barred him from Annapolis. The maximum age limit there was nineteen for freshmen, and Ike was twenty, just a few months too old.

Luckily, there was no such rule at West Point. On July 1, 1911, Ike found himself climbing the hill to the Point — the same hill that Ulysses Grant had climbed seventy-two years before.

The always popular Ike made many friends during his plebe (freshman) year and did well in his studies. He stood fifty-seventh in a class of 212, but he was far more interested in becoming the best football player in it.

By the end of his plebe year he had achieved that goal — and more. He made a name for himself not only in football but in baseball, boxing, and track.

He went out for the varsity football team in the fall of 1912, and before the first game was played sports writers from eastern newspapers were predicting great things for him. They called him the "huge Kansan" and described him as a "plunging halfback."

He had reached his full growth by that time. At twenty-one he weighed about 180 pounds and was just under six feet in height. His broad shoulders tapered down to a slender waist and his muscles were hard and smooth.

Ike worked long hours on the practice field and was picked by the coaches to share the left halfback position with Geoffrey Keyes, a senior who had been the team's star the year before. It is not often that a sophomore gets that far at West Point in his first try for the varsity, but Ike was too good for the bench. As it turned out, he started almost as many games as Keyes did.

He was a ferocious tackler and he blocked beautifully. He could punt and he ran with terrific drive through the line. He was at his

110

best, perhaps, as a linebacker. Charles Benedict supported Ike in backing up the Army's seven-man line. Often they would simultaneously tackle an opposing back who had smashed his way through the Army line.

Ike and his friendly rival, Geoffrey Keyes, alternated in starting the early-season games. Both played well and Ike, the newcomer, got some encouraging notices in the press. "One of the most promising backs in Eastern football," wrote the New York *Times* of the new star.

In midseason the Army played Carlisle, an Indian school in Pennsylvania that was captained by the great Olympic hero and All-American halfback, Jim Thorpe.* The magnificent Indian was a one-man team. He could do everything on the football field and was unstoppable when he had the ball.

Against the Army he played one of the best games of his career. He tore the line to shreds, swept the ends, and made a series of spectacular runs. One time when Jim broke through the line, Ike and Benedict hit him together, one high and one low, and stretched him out on the turf. They thought that for once they had stopped him, but Jim got to his feet after a short time out and made ten yards on the next play.

Thorpe ran wild after that. There was no stopping him. Once again, though, Ike and Benedict saw their chance to "high-low" the Indian with a double tackle. They had him cornered and both dived for him, but Jim stopped short in his tracks and the two cadets crashed head on. The Indian kept going. Ike and Benedict lay flat on the ground, unconscious. Both were taken out of the game and Carlisle went on to win, 27-6. When it was over the entire Cadet Corps rose in the stands and gave the Indian a rousing ovation.

In later life Jim Thorpe always said that this was the best game he ever played. He was asked if he remembered playing against a

---

* Thorpe, a Sac and Fox Indian, is generally considered to be the greatest all-around athlete who ever lived. In the 1912 Olympics he won the Pentathlon and the Decathlon, a feat that has never been duplicated. He was All-America halfback in 1911 and 1912 and his name appears on every all-time, All-America team that experts have picked since his time. Following his brilliant college football career, he was an outstanding professional football player for many years. He also played major-league baseball (for eight years) with the New York Giants and the Boston Braves. When he died in 1953 the State of Pennsylvania named a town in his honor. It is Jim Thorpe, Pa.

cadet named Eisenhower. Jim nodded and said, "Good linebacker."

Ike had started in the Carlisle game and he was again in the lineup for the opening kickoff the following week against Tufts. He was now a regular and he would undoubtedly have developed into one of the Army's finest backs had it not been for a stroke of bad luck. He broke his knee and was carried off the field.

Dr. Charles Keller, the chief surgeon, examined the knee. He shook his head sadly when Ike, although in great pain, asked him if he would be able to play in the Navy game. "Not this year," said the doctor. "Maybe never. You'll have to go to the hospital and lie flat on your back for several weeks."

That was the last football game Ike ever played. The weakened knee was later made worse by an accident in the riding hall and Ike knew that he was finished as a football player. It was the most bitter disappointment of his life.

He became a cheer leader so that he could stay close to the game. It was the next best thing to playing but, of course, it wasn't the same. He tried to forget about the knee and his lost dream of glory but it was difficult. He was dispirited at times.

A description of Ike written in the 1915 *Howitzer,* an Academy publication, shows that his classmates were aware of his disappointment. It read in part: ". . . poor Dwight merely consents to exist until graduation shall set him free. At one time he threatened to get interested in life and won his 'A' by being the most promising back in Eastern football — but the Tufts game broke his knee and the promise."

Although Ike was immensely popular at West Point, his record there did not indicate that he would become famous in later life. Off the football field he was not among the lofty. The highest rank he held in the Cadet Corps was color sergeant. Scholastically he was just above the middle of his class when he graduated in 1915. He stood sixty-first in a class of 164. In deportment he was in the lower half, standing ninety-fifth.

Ike gathered more than his share of demerits during his four years at the Point, but his offenses were always trivial, never serious. He would be late for drill, or forget to bring a certain book to class, or be reported for an untidy room. He never once broke the Army's Code of Honor, which concerns lying and cheating.

112

President Dwight Eisenhower and Vice President Richard Nixon in an electric golf cart after a round of golf at the Burning Tree Country Club.

Promotions were slow in the Army between the two World Wars. Although Ike became a major five years after he graduated, he remained in that rank for the next sixteen years, until 1936, when he was forty-six years old.

Things happened rapidly after that as World War II approached. From a lieutenant colonel in 1941, Ike shot up to full general in less than two years. The promotion was well earned. In a competitive test of officers on the problems of Pacific strategy, his plan stood out above all the others.

Subsequently he was appointed by President Roosevelt as Supreme Commander for the invasion of Europe. This was the road that led to the White House.

Ike was the most sports-minded president since Teddy Roosevelt. He was a devoted angler and, like Hoover, he was a purist — a stream-wading flycaster. He was a fine shot with both pistol and shotgun. His favorite sport, however, was golf. During his eight years in the White House (1953-1961) he played the game more often and more skillfully than any other president before him. He played it hard and to win, just as he had played all the games of his boyhood and youth.

John Fitzgerald Kennedy, the ill-starred President who succeeded Eisenhower, stood high on the presidential list as a sports lover. He was an enthusiastic and well-informed fan on all major sports, and he was also a participant when his ailing back permitted.

Jack, as the President was known to his friends, was the son of Joseph P. Kennedy, who amassed an incredible fortune of some two hundred million dollars. Jack was one of nine children, and his parents did everything they could to introduce them to all forms of athletics, the girls included.

The Kennedys lived in large homes in various places — in Bronxville, New York, Hyannis Port at Cape Cod in Massachusetts, and Palm Beach, Florida. No matter where they lived there were always tennis courts on the place or nearby, and swimming pools and facilities for sailing.

There were enough Kennedy youngsters around for a game of doubles in tennis or a handicap race of so many laps in the pool. There were even enough for a game of touch football, which the girls learned to play. They could pass, kick, and run almost as well as their brothers.

At the Palm Beach ocean-front estate a professional was engaged to encourage the children in athletics and to see that they kept in good physical shape. He taught them to swim and dive and led them in setting-up exercises. He put boxing gloves on with the boys and taught them self-defense.

It is small wonder that the Kennedys grew up with a strong love of sports. They were almost a sports world unto themselves. They went sailing together, played golf against each other, and rode horseback in a group. A family friend described them as "the most competitive and at the same time the most united family" that she had ever seen.

John F. Kennedy on 1937 Harvard Freshman Swimming Team. Third from left, top row.

John F. Kennedy, aged 10, on the Dexter School Football Team, Brookline, Mass.

Jack, the second oldest of the four boys, was the least rugged of the lot. He was skinny and inclined to be sickly as a youngster but he tried his best to make the grade in football, baseball, and swimming — and never quite made it.

He got his first setback at the age of thirteen at Canterbury School in Connecticut when he went out for football but was turned down because he was too light. Later at Choate School, which is also in Connecticut, he tried football again but he was not big enough for the varsity. Undaunted, he went out for intramural football and made a team, playing tackle and end against boys of his own size.

His coaches remember him as an eager and scrappy player, yet reluctant to try very hard in practice. The Choate yearbook called him "a tiger on defense."

As a senior at Choate, Jack played a lot of golf and tennis but he was not a member of the school teams in these sports. He was eighteen years old, nearly six feet tall, and he weighed about 155 pounds. He was handsome, likeable, intelligent, and greatly respected by his classmates. Prophetically, they voted him the person "most likely to succeed."

In the fall of 1935 Jack entered Princeton but he was there for only one term. A severe attack of jaundice laid him low and he left college when he recovered. The following year he went to Harvard as a freshman.

His athletic career there was about the same as it had been at Choate. Again he went out for football but he could not make the varsity. He had to settle for the junior varsity. It was in his sophomore year in 1937 during a scrimmage with the jayvees against the varsity that Kennedy injured his back, an ailment that caused him frequent discomfort the rest of his life.*

Jack took part in intramural sports whenever he could. He played softball and hockey and swam for Winthrop House, his dormitory residence. Recalling those days at Harvard, he said: "I wasn't a terribly good athlete but I participated."

There is no doubt that he was more brilliant in studies than in sports. He graduated *cum laude* in three and a half years, and at

---

* From time to time, the President's back hurt him so much that he could not play golf, touch football, dive in the White House pool, or even lift his children.

the suggestion of Arthur Krock of the New York *Times*, he expanded his thesis into a book, *Why England Slept*. It became an immediate best seller.

Jack's parents thought that he would most likely become a teacher or writer, but the war changed all that. Despite his chronically ailing back, he passed the Navy's fitness tests by taking special exercises and was assigned to the South Pacific with the rank of lieutenant.

In the Solomons a Jap destroyer ran down his PT boat and sliced it in two, hurling Kennedy to the deck. Although he was in agony he managed to rescue his crew. With the strap of one man's life jacket in his teeth, Kennedy swam for five hours and towed him to the nearest land. Several days later the marooned group was found and brought to safety.

Kennedy emerged from the war a genuine hero. He was discharged in 1945, after the Navy gave him a back operation, and decided to go into politics. He served three terms in Congress and was elected to the United States Senate in 1953. Seven years later he was elected president.

At forty-three he was the youngest man ever elected to the presidency and the first of Roman Catholic faith.

Kennedy's enthusiasm for sports did not change when he entered the White House. He was still an ardent baseball, football, and boxing fan. When he attended the Army-Navy game or any other football contest, his interest was more than ceremonial or political. He knew the game thoroughly and enjoyed every minute of it, even though he often had to sit in a soft leather armchair because of his bad back.

Kennedy followed major-league baseball and knew the standings of the clubs in both leagues, as well as the batting averages of the top hitters. His favorite player was Stan Musial.

He swam in the White House pool daily when he was in Washington. He used to play golf regularly, usually shooting in the seventies, but gave it up on doctor's orders after aggravating his old back injury during a tree-planting ceremony in Ottawa in May, 1961.

He did not play again until the summer of 1963, when he tried a few holes at Hyannis Port in company with Mrs. Kennedy and her large black German shepherd dog, Clipper.

The President also found time for sailing and salt-water fishing in Florida and on Cape Cod. He had his own sailboat, a twenty-four-foot sloop named *Victura*, which he often skippered.

One of his favorite recreations was going aboard the presidential yacht, *Honey Fitz*, in company with various members of the large Kennedy family. He named the palatial craft in honor of his maternal grandfather, John F. (Honey Fitz) Fitzgerald, who was mayor of Boston years ago.

The President's love of sports was shared by his wife, the former Jacqueline Bouvier, a dark-eyed beauty who was by all odds the most athletic First Lady in White House history. A horsewoman of the first order, she had her own pony at the age of six, and by twelve she was riding in horse shows. She is a follower of the hounds and often goes fox hunting in Virginia. She is a good tennis player, a golfer, and a better-than-average water skier. She even played touch football, but after breaking an ankle in a Kennedy family scrimmage, she gave up the game for good.

John F. Kennedy and his fiancée, Jacqueline Bouvier, about to start a tennis game.

President John F. Kennedy and his wife sailing off Hyannis Port, Mass.

The President used to sit in a special rocking chair which was designed to ease his back. From it came many of his directives and suggestions. In the winter of 1963 a thought expressed by the President as he sat in the rocking chair started a national fad.

It all began with an old order signed by Teddy Roosevelt that a Marine Corps general came across by chance. The order, dated 1908, set forth that every Marine captain and lieutenant should be able to march fifty miles in twenty hours (over a three-day period). The general, knowing that President Kennedy was a strong advocate of physical fitness, thought that he might be interested in it and passed it on to him.

Kennedy read it and said, "It would be interesting to know how well our present-day officers could perform the tests specified by President Roosevelt."

119

It was merely an idle thought of Kennedy's, not an order. He was only thinking out loud. But the Marine general did not see it that way. He ordered a division of Marines to take the fifty-mile hike and prove they were the equal of the old Corps of Roosevelt's day.

That started things. The President's brother, Attorney General Robert F. (Bobby) Kennedy, an ex-Harvard football player,* set out with four aides one frosty morning at dawn and completed the hike alone. His companions dropped out one by one.

Everybody seemed to fall into step after that. All over the country Boy Scouts took the hike and walked their scoutmasters into the ground. College students, pretty secretaries, politicians, and businessmen trudged along. At Stanford University students hiked in sweatshirts and derbies. In Seattle a group of boys and girls went the distance on roller skates. In California 400 high school students set out on the hike and ninety-seven of them finished, including nineteen girls.

Newsweek magazine, commenting on the fad, stated: "With one idle remark, Mr. Kennedy put more vigor into Americans than his Council on Physical Fitness had done in six and a half years of preachment."

San Francisco's *News-Call Bulletin* said: "For good or bad, one of President Kennedy's campaign promises has come true. He's surely got the country moving again."

From his rocking chair, President Kennedy wondered at all the hubbub and probably wished that he could have taken the hike, too. The limitations on his own participation in athletics were necessary, but even a less active role was not without its dangers.

One year when Kennedy was attending an Army-Navy football game in Philadelphia an incident occurred that made many people shudder. It happened as the President was walking across the field at half-time. Suddenly a man burst through the cordon of cadets and midshipmen accompanying Kennedy and came within a foot of putting his hands on him. Just as suddenly the man was subdued by Secret Service guards.

* All four Kennedy brothers went out for football at Harvard. Joseph, Jr., the oldest (who was killed over Europe as a World War II flyer), made the varsity squad but never earned his letter. Jack rose no higher than the jayvees. Bobby won his H three years, made first string his senior year. The youngest brother, Edward M. (Teddy), made end on the first team his senior year and earned his letter. In 1911 their father, Joseph, Sr., won his H in baseball.

President Kennedy drives off at the Hyannis Port Golf Club on Cape Cod for a short round of golf. Photograph was taken in the summer of 1963.

It was apparent to all who witnessed the event that the man was drunk. Undoubtedly he had no intention of harming the President. Nevertheless, the implication was frightening. If a harmless drunk could get that close to the President, what could a man with purpose and murder in his heart do — a maniac, for example, bent on destroying the Chief Executive?

The answer came with terrifying swiftness on Friday, November 22, 1963 when a sniper, firing from the sixth floor of a building in Dallas, Texas, sent two rifle bullets through the President's brain and throat as he was riding in a motorcade in the downtown section of the city.

Instantly the news of the assassination was flashed across the country; it hit the the American people like a shock wave. Millions

Mrs. Kennedy and John Jr. on "Sardar" with Caroline alongside on "Macaroni."

were stunned, bewildered, angered, and saddened. It did not seem possible that this tanned and vigorous young man could be obliterated in the brief span of a few minutes.

The nation went into mourning. Business was suspended, the stock exchanges closed down, television and theatrical shows were cancelled, and most sporting events were either postponed or given up.

The President died the day before the Saturday that should have been the last full day of the college football season. Most college presidents called off the final games, or had them postponed. Harvard and Yale, on the eve of their eightieth game, were the first to announce that they would not play. The rest of the Ivy League quickly followed suit. Their final games were played a week later than scheduled, as was the Army-Navy game. (This game might have been cancelled had it not been for members of the Kennedy family who requested that it be played.)

A few colleges decided to play the day after the President died anyway. Most of these were the football factories of the south, such as Auburn, Florida State, Miami, Florida, Tennessee, Kentucky

Jacqueline Kennedy water-skiing with astronaut John Glenn, who has just taken a spill. See splash at right.

and North Carolina State. Nebraska and Oklahoma, thirsting for an Orange Bowl bid, elected to play.

On Sunday the American Football League cancelled all of its games. However, the other professional circuit, the National Football League, hung up the business-as-usual sign. For so doing the League President, Pete Rozelle, was bitterly assailed in many sports pages. "For that exercise in tasteless stupidity there is neither excuse nor defense," wrote sports columnist Red Smith.

In a final tribute to President Kennedy, *Sports Illustrated* magazine published an article entitled "The President Who Loved Sport," in which it was pointed out that Kennedy had a consuming, lifelong dedication to sports and fitness. He was a well-informed fan on all phases of sport, the article stated, and he was also a participant and a hero-worshiper of sports figures.

The one thing that he did not like about sport was the practice of what he called "spectating" which to him meant sitting in front of a television set on a fine day and watching a game. The President, who was a doer, had contempt for this kind of a sports fan. He strongly believed, said *Sports Illustrated*, in these words of Homer: "There is no greater glory for a man while yet he lives than that which he achieves by his own hands and feet."

Two cars behind the presidential limousine in the motorcade on that fateful day in Dallas was an open convertible carrying Vice President Lyndon B. Johnson and his wife, Lady Bird (a nickname given her by a Negro nurse when she was an infant). The second car in line bristled with Secret Service men.

Following the assassin's shots these three cars sped to the hospital and arrived within seconds of each other. There Kennedy died and just 107 minutes later Lyndon Johnson took the oath of office and became the thirty-sixth President of the United States.

The entire ceremony lasted only two minutes. It was performed aboard the presidential airplane, Air Force One, and, incidentally, was administered by Federal Judge Sarah T. Hughes, the first woman in history to swear in a United States president.

Lyndon Baines Johnson, a big six-foot, three-inch Texan who measures up to Washington and Lincoln in size, had little opportunity for sports in his youth and today he has only a mild interest in them.

President Johnson waving to friends on the LBJ Ranch.

Born on August 27, 1908 in a frame house on the banks of the Pedernales River near Stonewall in Central Texas, Johnson came from a poor family and had to work when he was a boy. However, like all Texas ranch boys he found time to shoot and ride horseback.

He attended high school in nearby Johnson City (named for his grandfather, who founded it) and following his graduation he spent three years at various odd jobs. He worked on ranches, became a fruit picker, and roamed about the Southwest. He was on a road building gang for a year.

He decided to continue his education and entered Southwest Texas State Teachers College at San Marcos in 1927. He graduated in 1930, finishing the four-year course in three years. He is remembered there as a hard worker and a star on the college debating team — not as an athlete.

A friendly man with a broad open face that seems to be made for the ten-gallon Texas hat he often wears, Johnson rose up through the political ranks and his wealth increased as he did. He served in the House of Representatives, as a United States Senator, Majority Leader of the Senate and Vice President. Among his colleagues he was highly respected and known as a hard worker.

It was possibly his devotion to strenuous labor that contributed to the severe heart attack he suffered on July 2, 1955, when he was forty-six years old. "It was," he says, "as bad an attack as a man could have and live."

Up to that time he had been a heavy smoker, averaging three packs of cigarettes a day. He smoked his last cigarette just before he was put under an oxygen tent in the Naval Medical Center at Bethesda, Maryland.

Since then he has made other sensible adjustments, such as cutting down on fattening foods and drinking decaffeined coffee.

President Johnson enjoys swimming. He had a heated pool in his Washington home and there is another one in Texas on his LBJ ranch which is about sixty-five miles from Austin.

President Johnson likes to hunt deer when he is on his ranch. He often goes horseback riding on inspection tours to see the sheep and cattle on his lands. He does setting-up exercises in the mornings and has frequent massages.

In recent years he has taken up boating as a hobby, plying his motorboat up and down the Pedernales River that runs in front of his ranch house. The river continues on to a series of lakes around Austin.

President Johnson on horseback in front of his Texas ranchhouse.

Appendix

SPORTS OF THE PRESIDENTS
(Participant and Spectator)

BASEBALL	Grant, Taft, Wilson, Hoover, Eisenhower, Kennedy.
BILLIARDS	Washington, J. Q. Adams, Lincoln, Garfield, Cleveland.
BOATING	L. B. Johnson
BOXING	T. Roosevelt, Eisenhower.
CANOEING	Washington, Arthur, F. D. Roosevelt.
COCKFIGHTING	Washington, Jackson, Lincoln.
CROQUET	Hayes.
DRIVING (Horses)	Grant, Hayes, T. Roosevelt.
EXPLORING	Washington, T. Roosevelt.
FISHING	Washington, Jefferson, Monroe, Arthur, Benjamin Harrison, Cleveland, McKinley, Coolidge, Hoover, F. D. Roosevelt, Truman, Eisenhower, Kennedy, L. B. Johnson.
FOOTBALL	John Adams, Wilson, Hoover, F. D. Roosevelt, Eisenhower, Kennedy.
GOLF	McKinley, Taft, Wilson, Harding, F. D. Roosevelt, Eisenhower, Kennedy, L. B. Johnson.
HORSERACING	Washington, Jefferson, J. Q. Adams, Jackson, Grant.
HUNTING	Washington, John Adams, Monroe, Taylor, Buchanan, Hayes, Arthur, Cleveland, Benjamin Harrison, T. Roosevelt, Eisenhower, L. B. Johnson.
JUJITSU	T. Roosevelt.
MARBLES	Tyler, Lincoln.
MECHANICAL HORSE	Coolidge.

SPORTS OF THE PRESIDENTS
(Participant and Spectator)

MEDICINE BALL	Hoover.
MOUNTAIN CLIMBING	T. Roosevelt.
POLO	T. Roosevelt.
RIDING	Washington, John Adams, Jefferson, Monroe, J. Q. Adams, Jackson, Van Buren, Wm. H. Harrison, Tyler, Taylor, Grant, Garfield, McKinley, T. Roosevelt, Taft, Wilson, Harding, F. D. Roosevelt, Eisenhower, L. B. Johnson.
ROWING	T. Roosevelt, F. D. Roosevelt.
RUNNING	Jefferson, F. D. Roosevelt.
SAILING	F. D. Roosevelt, Kennedy.
SHOOTING (Clay Pigeons)	Coolidge.
SKATING	John Adams, Grant, Benjamin Harrison, McKinley.
SWIMMING	John Adams, Jefferson, Monroe, J. Q. Adams, Taylor, Pierce, Grant, Arthur, McKinley, F. D. Roosevelt, Kennedy, L. B. Johnson.
TABLE TENNIS	Harding.
TENNIS	T. Roosevelt, Harding, Kennedy.
TOUCH FOOTBALL	Kennedy.
TOWN BALL (Early Baseball)	John Adams, Benjamin Harrison.
WALKING	Jefferson, Madison, J. Q. Adams, Van Buren, Pierce, Buchanan, Lincoln, Garfield, McKinley, T. Roosevelt, Wilson, Coolidge, Truman, L. B. Johnson.
WEIGHT LIFTING	Lincoln.
WRESTLING	Lincoln, T. Roosevelt.

President	Term of Office	Height	Weight (Approximate)	Physical Characteristics
George Washington (1732-1799)	1789-1797	6' 3"	190 lbs.	Reddish hair; blue eyes; pock-marked face; false teeth; erect carriage; large hands and feet.
John Adams (1735-1826)	1797-1801	5' 7"	170 lbs.	Bald; chubby.
Thomas Jefferson (1743-1826)	1801-1809	6' 2¼"	180 lbs.	Reddish hair; sharp featured.
James Madison (1751-1836)	1809-1817	5' 4"	100 lbs.	(Shortest president) Slight frame; light hair; blue eyes; small voice.
James Monroe (1758-1831)	1817-1825	6'	185 lbs.	Blue eyes; broad shoulder rugged physique.
John Quincy Adams (1767-1848)	1825-1829	5' 7"	170 lbs.	Bald; chubby.
Andrew Jackson (1767-1845)	1829-1837	6' 1"	150 lbs.	Bushy gray hair and eyebrows; blue eyes; thin.
Martin Van Buren (1782-1862)	1837-1841	5' 6"	140 lbs.	Small slight build; erect carriage.
William Henry Harrison (1773-1841)	1841-	5' 11"	165 lbs.	Tall; slim; erect.

Sports and Activities	Religion	College and Graduating Class	Age at Death
Billiards, canoeing, cockfighting, exploring, fishing, horse racing, hunting, riding.	Episcopalian		67 Years 295 Days
Football, hunting, riding, skating, swimming, town ball.	Unitarian	Harvard 1775	90 Years 247 Days
Fishing, horse racing, riding, running, swimming, walking.	Deist	William and Mary 1762	83 Years 82 Days
Walking.	Episcopalian	Princeton 1771	85 Years 104 Days
Fishing, hunting, riding, swimming.	Episcopalian	William and Mary 1776	73 Years 67 Days
Billiards, horse racing, riding, swimming, walking.	Unitarian	Harvard 1787	80 Years 227 Days
Cockfighting, horse racing, riding.	Presbyterian		78 Years 85 Days
Riding, walking.	Reformed Dutch		79 Years 231 Days
Riding.	Episcopalian	Hampden Sydney (Did not graduate)	68 Years 54 Days

President	Term of Office	Height	Weight (Approximate)	Physical Characteristics
John Tyler (1790-1862)	1841-1845	6'	170 lbs.	Tall; thin; brown hair; blue eyes; prominent nose.
James K. Polk (1795-1849)	1845-1849	5' 8"	137 lbs.	Frail and sickly; thin; gray eyes; sharp features.
Zachary Taylor (1784-1850)	1849-1850	5' 8"	170 lbs.	Dark hair; gray eyes; ruddy; short legs.
Millard Fillmore (1800-1874)	1850-1853	5' 9"	175 lbs.	Well proportioned body; grayish hair; blue eyes.
Franklin Pierce (1804-1869)	1853-1857	5' 10"	170 lbs.	Erect military bearing; small but strong features; blue eyes.
James Buchanan (1791-1868)	1857-1861	6'	185 lbs.	Pudgy; short neck; poor eyesight; light complexion.
Abraham Lincoln (1809-1865)	1861-1865	6' 4"	180 lbs.	(Tallest president) Tall and thin; gray eyes; black hair; mole on cheek; very strong features.
Andrew Johnson (1808-1875)	1865-1869	5' 10"	180 lbs.	High forehead; brown hair; stocky build.
Ulysses S. Grant (1822-1885)	1869-1877	5' 8"	165 lbs.	Short and chunky; large head; firm-set mouth; beard.
Rutherford B. Hayes (1822-1893)	1877-1881	5' 8½"	170 lbs.	Blue eyes; brown hair and beard; mild voice.

Sports and Activities	Religion	College and Graduating Class	Age at Death
Marbles, riding.	Episcopalian	William and Mary 1807	71 Years 295 Days
None.	Methodist	North Carolina 1818	53 Years 225 Days
Hunting, riding, swimming.	Episcopalian		65 Years 227 Days
None.	Unitarian		74 Years 60 Days
Swimming, walking.	Episcopalian	Bowdoin 1824	64 Years 319 Days
Hunting, walking.	Presbyterian	Dickinson 1809	77 Years 39 Days
Billiards, cockfighting, marbles, walking, weight lifting, wrestling.	Attended but never joined Presbyterian Church		56 Years 62 Days
None.	Methodist		66 Years 214 Days
Baseball, driving, horse racing, skating, swimming.	Methodist	U. S. Military Academy 1843	63 Years 87 Days
Croquet, driving, hunting.	Attended but never joined Methodist Church	Kenyon 1842	70 Years 105 Days

President	Term of Office	Height	Weight (Approximate)	Physical Characteristics
James A. Garfield (1831-1881)	1881-	6'	185 lbs.	Blue eyes; brown hair and beard; broad shoulders; large frame; left handed.
Chester A. Arthur (1830-1886)	1881-1885	6' 2"	225 lbs.	Handsome; big frame; full side whiskers and mustache.
Grover Cleveland (1837-1908)	1885-1889 1893-1897	5' 11"	260 lbs.	Fat; baldish; drooping mustache; graying hair; heavy jowls; short neck.
Benjamin Harrison (1833-1901)	1889-1893	5' 6"	140 lbs.	Blond; blue eyes; full beard; small frame; short legs.
William McKinley (1843-1901)	1897-1901	5' 7"	165 lbs.	Stocky; high forehead; prominent chin.
Theodore Roosevelt (1858-1919)	1901-1909	5' 10"	170 lbs.	Eyeglasses with thick lenses; bushy mustache; prominent teeth; high voice
William Howard Taft (1857-1930)	1909-1913	6'	300-350 lbs.	(Heaviest president) Enormous frame; fat; rosy complexion; deep-set eyes turned-up mustache.
Woodrow Wilson (1856-1924)	1913-1921	5' 11"	175 lbs.	Prominent chin; clean cut, ascetic face; eyeglasses.

Sports and Activities	Religion	College and Graduating Class	Age at Death
Billiards, riding, walking.	Disciples of Christ	Williams 1856	49 Years 304 Days
Canoeing, fishing, hunting, swimming.	Episcopalian	Union 1848	56 Years 44 Days
Billiards, fishing, hunting.	Presbyterian		71 Years 98 Days
Hunting; skating, fishing, town ball.	Presbyterian	Miami 1852	67 Years 205 Days
Fishing, riding, golf, skating, swimming, walking.	Methodist	Allegheny (Did not graduate)	58 Years 228 Days
Boxing, driving, exploring, hunting, jujitsu, mountain climbing, polo, riding, rowing, tennis, walking, wrestling.	Reformed Dutch	Harvard 1880	60 Years 71 Days
Baseball, golf, riding.	Unitarian	Yale 1878	72 Years 174 Days
Baseball, football, golf, riding, walking.	Presbyterian	Princeton 1879	67 Years 37 Days

President	Term of Office	Height	Weight (Approximate)	Physical Characteristics
Warren G. Harding (1865-1923)	1921-1923	6'	200 lbs.	Handsome; high forehead; graying hair; bushy eyebrows.
Calvin Coolidge (1872-1933)	1923-1929	5' 9"	150 lbs.	Wide forehead; thin nose; tightly set lips; grim expression; sandy hair; brown eyes.
Herbert C. Hoover (1874-)	1929-1933	5' 11"	190 lbs.	Square-faced; heavy set; ruddy complexion.
Franklin Delano Roosevelt (1882-1945)	1933-1945	6' 2"	188 lbs.	High forehead; gray hair; wore reading glasses; wore braces on legs.
Harry S Truman (1884-)	1945-1953	5' 9"	167 lbs.	Hazel eyes; gray hair; eyeglasses.
Dwight D. Eisenhower (1890-)	1953-1961	5' 10½"	180 lbs.	Bald with fringes of white hair; blue eyes; engaging smile.
John Fitzgerald Kennedy (1917-1963)	1961-1963	6'	175 lbs.	Gray-blue eyes; straight mouth; a profusion of hair.
Lyndon Baines Johnson (1908-)	1963-	6' 3"	190 lbs.	Rugged countenance; graying hair, brown eyes; Southern accent.

Sports and Activities	Religion	College and Graduating Class	Age at Death
Golf, riding, table tennis, tennis.	Baptist		57 Years 273 Days
Fishing, mechanical horse, shooting (clay pigeons), walking.	Congrega-tionalist	Amherst 1895	60 Years 185 Days
Baseball, fishing, football, medicine ball.	Friends (Quaker)	Stanford 1895	
Canoeing, fishing, football, golf, riding, rowing, running, sailing, swimming.	Episcopalian	Harvard 1903	63 Years 72 Days
Fishing, walking.	Baptist		
Baseball, boxing, fishing, football, golf, hunting, riding.	Presbyterian	U. S. Military Academy 1915	
Baseball, fishing, football, golf, sailing, swimming, tennis, touch football.	Roman Catholic	Harvard 1940	46 Years 177 Days
Boating, golf, hunting, riding, swimming, walking.	Disciples of Christ	Southwest Texas State Teachers College 1930	

PICTURE CREDITS

New York Public Library, 8, 10, 13, 21, 36, 55

Frick Art Reference Library, 11

Drawn especially for this book by Joshua Tolford, 15, 38, 42, 45

American Museum of Natural History, 17

The Old Print Shop, New York, 18

Independence Hall (Philadelphia) Collection, 25

Author's Collection, 26, 28, 31, 35, 86, 88, 91, 94

Metropolitan Museum of Art, 33

McClure's Magazine, July 1897, 44, 58

Harper's Weekly, December 12, 1868, 49

Harper's Weekly, April 17, 1869, 62

University of Michigan Museum of Art, 50

Ladies' Home Journal, April 1901, 53

Library of Congress, 57

New-York Historical Society, 63

"Fishing and Shooting Sketches" by Grover Cleveland, 69

Leslie's Illustrated Weekly, February 10, 1866, 70

Theodore Roosevelt Association, 74, 75, 82

Cartoons by McCutcheon, 78

Judge, 1905, 81

Life, 1904, 80

National Baseball Museum, Cooperstown, N.Y., 85, 86

Puck, February 21, 1914, 90

Smithsonian Institution, 98

Franklin D. Roosevelt Library, 103, 105

European, 106

United Press International, 109, 113, 115, 118, 119, 122, 123, 125, 127

SELECTED BIBLIOGRAPHY

Some of the material in this book was gleaned from magazine articles and books written by the author. These include a series of *Sports Illustrated* magazine articles entitled *Sports of the Presidents* in which the following chief executives were treated: Washington, Jackson, Cleveland, Grant, and Wilson. The books are *Pictorial History of American Sports* (1952), *Yesterday in Sports* (1956), and *Pictorial History of American Presidents* (1962), the last-named in collaboration with my wife, Alice Rand Durant. All three were published by A. S. Barnes & Co., Inc.

Bishop, Joseph B.: *Theodore Roosevelt* (Charles Scribner's Sons — 1925)

Bowen, Catherine Drinker: *John Adams and the American Revolution* (Little, Brown & Co. — 1950)

Butt, Archibald W.: *Taft and Roosevelt* (Vols. I & II) (Doubleday, Doran & Co. — 1930)

Butterfield, Roger: *The American Past* (Simon & Schuster, Inc. — 1947)

Carmer, Carl: *Cavalcade of America* (Crown Publishers, Inc. — 1956)

Cleveland, Grover: *Fishing and Shooting Sketches* (Outing Publishing Co. — 1907)

Coffin, Charles C.: *Building the Nation* (Harper & Brothers — 1883)

Colman, Edna M.: *Seventy-Five Years of White House Gossip* (Doubleday, Page & Co. — 1926)

Davidson, Marshall B.: *Life in America* (Vols. I & II) (Houghton Mifflin Co. — 1951)

Davis, Kenneth S.: *Soldier of Democracy* (Doubleday, Doran & Co. — 1945)

Dulles, Foster Rhea: *America Learns to Play* (Smith, Peter — 1940)

Fraser, Hugh Russell: *Democracy in the Making* (The Bobbs-Merrill Co., Inc. — 1938)

Furman, Bess: *White House Profile* (The Bobbs-Merrill Co., Inc. — 1951)

Graham, Alberta Powell: *Thirty-three Roads to the White House* (Thomas Nelson & Sons — 1944)

Gunther, John: *Roosevelt in Retrospect* (Harper & Brothers — 1950)

Hagedorn, Herman: *Boy's Life of Theodore Roosevelt* (Harper & Brothers — 1918)

Hatch, Alden: *General Ike* (Henry Holt & Co. — 1945)

Henderson, Robert W.: *Early American Sport* (A. S. Barnes & Co., Inc. — 1953)

Hoover, Herbert: *Fishing for Fun* (Random House, Inc. — 1963)

Isely, Bliss: *The Presidents, Men of Faith* (W. A. Wilde Co. — 1954)

James, Marquis: *The Life of Andrew Jackson* (The Bobbs-Merrill Co., Inc. — 1938)

Jensen, Amy LaFollette: *The White House and Its Thirty-Two Families* (McGraw-Hill Book Co. — 1958)

Kane, Joseph: *Facts About the Presidents* (H. W. Wilson Co. — 1960)

Kouwenhoven, John: *Adventures of America, 1857-1900* (Harper & Brothers — 1938)

Krout, John Allen: *Annals of American Sport, Pageant of America,* Vol. XV (Yale University Press — 1929)

Lee, Bruce: *JFK: Boyhood to the White House* (Fawcett Books — 1961)

Lorant, Stefan: *The Presidency* (The Macmillan Company — 1951)

Lorant, Stefan: *Lincoln, A Picture Story of His Life* (Harper & Brothers — 1952)

McConnell, Burt Morton: *The White House* (Studio Publications in association with Viking Press — 1954)

Milhollen, H., and M. Kaplan: *Presidents on Parade* (The Macmillan Company — 1948)

Morgan, James: *Our Presidents* (The Macmillan Company — 1954)

Morrel, Martha McB.: *Young Hickory* (E. P. Dutton & Co., Inc. — 1949)

Mowry, George E.: *The Era of Theodore Roosevelt, 1900-1912* (Harper & Brothers — 1958)

Nevins, Allan: *Grover Cleveland* (Dodd, Mead & Company — 1948)

Pringle, Henry F.: *The Life and Times of William Howard Taft* (Farrar & Rinehart — 1939)

Roosevelt, Theodore: *Theodore Roosevelt, An Autobiography* (The Macmillan Company — 1920)

Sandberg, Carl: *Abraham Lincoln* (Harcourt, Brace & Company, Inc. — 1925)

Sheean, Vincent: *Thomas Jefferson* (Random House, Inc. — 1953)

Smith, Bessie White: *The Boyhoods of the Presidents* (Lothrop, Lee & Shepard Co., Inc. — 1929)

142

Starling, Edmund W.: *Starling of the White House* (Simon & Schuster, Inc. — 1946)

Sullivan, Mark: *Our Times* (Vols. I-VI) (Charles Scribner's Sons — 1946)

Tebbel, John: *George Washington's America* (E. P. Dutton & Co., Inc. — 1954)

Thomas, Benjamin P.: *Abraham Lincoln* (Alfred A. Knopf, Inc. — 1952)

Truett, Randle B.: *The White House* (Hastings House, Publishers, Inc. — 1949)

Van Deusen, Glyndon G.: *The Jacksonian Era* (Harper & Brothers — 1950)

Weaver, Robert W.: *Amusements and Sports in American Life* (University of Chicago Press — 1939)

Weyand, Alexander M.: *Football Immortals* (The Macmillan Company — 1962)

White, William Allen: *Woodrow Wilson* (Houghton Mifflin Co. — 1924)

Woodward, W. E.: *Meet General Grant* (H. Liveright & Company — 1928)

Index